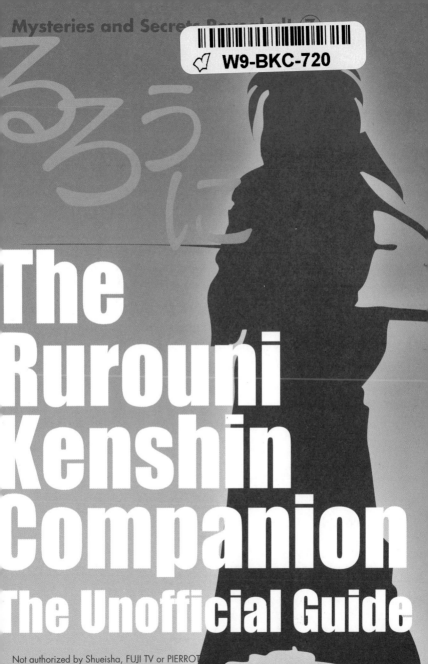

るろうに

The Rurouni Kenshin Companion

The Unofficial Guide

Not authorized by Shueisha, FUJI TV or PIERROT

cocoro books

Published by DH Publishing, Inc.
1-20-2-518,Higashiikebukuro, Toshima-Ku,
Tokyo 170-0013, Japan
www.dhp-online.com

cocoro books is an imprint of DH Publishing, Inc.

First published 2006

Text and illustrations © 2006 by DH Publishing, Inc.

Printed in CHINA

Printed by Miyuki Inter-Media Hong Kong, Inc.
Compiled by Kazuhisa Fujie and Walt Wyman
Publisher: Hiroshi Yokoi
Design: Kazuhisa Fujie
Editor: Kazuhisa Fujie
ISBN 1-932897-11-9

The Rurouni Kenshin Companion

How to Use
In this book, the seventh in the popular Mysteries and Secrets Revealed! anime series, you'll find everything you need to know about Rurouni Kenshin and much more! And it's so easy to use! Just follow the simple YuYu Hakusho code below and within a few hours you'll be an Demon World disciple.

Questions and Answers
Want to find out why who did what when and where? Then this is the book for you. 87 questions and detailed answers on every Rurouni Kenshin topic, from Spirit Detectives and Saint Beasts to fighting techniques and territories.

Glossary
When you speak the lingo everything is so much easier. At the back of this book you'll find a glossary stuffed full of names, what they mean and which pages to find them on.

Keyword Index
Want to go straight to Sarayashiki Junior High? Then start at the alphabetical Keyword Index at the back of the book. There you'll find page links to every destination in the YuYu Hakusho worlds.

A Note on Translations
In most cases, translations for fighting techniques, items, etc. follow the Funimation translation (because it is further along in the story than the Viz manga translation). If the Viz manga terms are known too, they appear in parentheses, for example: Spirit Gun (Rei Gun).

In cases where no "official" translations could be found (at the time of this writing, neither the anime nor manga translations are complete), the term appears in Romanized Japanese (example: Jigen Tou). Character names are in the Japanese style (last name first), and follow Funimation spellings (with the exception of "Keiko").

Series Overview

The Rurouni Kenshin -Meiji Kenkyaku Romantan- manga series ran in Shukan Shonen Jump between 1994 and 1999. The anime series ran from Jan. 1, 1996 to Sep. 8, 1998 on the Fuji Television network. In the manga version, after the conclusion of the "Kyoto" story arc, the third "Jinchu" arc followed. However, the anime's third story was a completely original work called the "Fusui" arc. A Rurouni Kenshin movie was made in 1997, and 6 original videos have been released.

This book considers the manga to be the definitive work, so all explanations of the story are based on it. The anime was broadcast under the English name "SAMURAI X" abroad, but this book uses the title Rurouni Kenshin for both the manga and anime.

The story takes place in Japan during the early days of the Meiji Era (1868-1912). The main characters are fictional, but because the story is historical fiction, many real figures appear too. The main protagonist's name is Himura Kenshin (aka Hitokiri Battosai), a former Ishin supporter with a cross-shaped scar on his left cheek. Rounding out the cast are Kamiya Kasshin fighting style instructor Kamiya Kaoru (aka the Kenjutsu Komachi), fighter-for-hire Sagara Sanosuke, and Myojin Yahiko, a boy orphaned by the turmoil of the Meiji Ishin.

CONTENTS

Rival Character's Secrets

The Rurouni Kenshin Companion

Main Character's Secrets

Name: **Himura Kenshin**
Occupation: **Wanderer**

An Ishin patriot from Choshu. He uses an ancient style of sword fighting called the 'Hiten Mitsurugi-Ryu'. At the age of 14 his talents as a swordsman earned him 5 years of employment as a hitokiri (assassin). During the latter half of the Ishin, he was hired to protect allies from the pro-Bakufu forces, such as the Shinsengumi. Then came the decisive battles of the Boshin Wars, and it's during these that Kenshin disappears (after the victory at Toba Fushimi, the first battle). He was dubbed the Battosai ('master of sword-drawing') due to his mastery of sword-drawing techniques. Ten years later, he resurfaces as a wanderer. His real name is Shinta.

緋村剣心

01 What was the 'Bakumatsu'?

The period called the Bakumatsu lasted from 1853 to around 1868. During this time, Japan transformed from a feudal government system controlled by the Tokugawa Shogun (the Bakufu) to a new national system focused on the Emperor.

From 1603 onward, the Tokugawa Shogun ruled Japan. This period is known as the Edo Period (because Japan's capital was moved to the city of Edo). During this age, Japan's samurai stood at the top of the social hierarchy, while the Emperor's lineage had no real power.

The Tokugawa Shoguns followed a policy of isolation, which limited trade with other countries. For a long time Japan enjoyed relative stability and a flourishing domestic culture. However, in 1853, Commodore Perry, commander of the US East Indies Squadron, entered Uraga Bay with 4 ships - the Mississippi, Plymouth, Saratoga, and Susquehanna- and put ashore at present day Kurihama to press for the opening of Japan's ports. The threat of foreign cannons sent a tremor

See Glossary
Himura Kenshin

9

through Japan. The next year a treaty between Japan and the US was concluded. Thus, after a very long period of isolation, Japan was opend abruptly.

From that time onward, a great number of people believed that Japan had to unite in the face of the threat posed by colonial powers. These people thought that if Japan did not undergo a revolution and become a modernized nation led by the Emperor, the country would be subjugated by one of the strong Western powers (such as the US). The revolutionary group is often referred to as the 'Ishin Shishi' (Ishin patriots).

In the Rurouni Kenshin universe, Kenshin is a former 'hitokiri' (assassin) for the Ishin Shishi, whose job was the elimination of Bakufu officials. In the end, the revolution succeeded and from 1868 the Emperor became the head of a new national government (although his role was symbolic -the real political power was wielded by a group of oligarchs). The years of chaos leading up to the revolution are referred to as the 'Bakumatsu'.

See questions
2

02 What is a 'hitokiri'?

This word (written 人斬り) literally means 'person cutter'. In other words, a hitokiri is a paid hit man. From 1863 to 1868, Kenshin worked for the Ishin faction as a hitokiri, eliminating Bakufu officials. However, being a former assassin doesn't necessarily make him a bad person. In that era, conventional wisdom dictated that killing was sometimes inevitable. For Kenshin's part, he wanted to help create a better country, and would kill those who obstructed 'justice'. Normally, as an assassin who killed in secret, Kenshin's name shouldn't have been widely known. However, he spent the latter half of his 6 year Ishin career protecting others from the pro-Bakufu faction's swords. His prowess with the blade made an indelible impression on those he protected, and thus the legend of the 'Hitokiri Battosai' was talked about for long after.

See Glossary
Himura Kenshin

03 When and why does Kenshin become an assassin?

At one point in the story, Sanosuke looks into Kenshin's past work for the Ishin faction. He learns that Kenshin became an assassin at 14. His master, Hiko Seijuro, confirms this. Kenshin met master Hiko Seijuro at the age of 10. Hiko saves Kenshin as he's being robbed, and we learn that Kenshin's name was originally Shinta. Hiko recommended the boy change his name to 'Kenshin', because it's more intimidating. Kenshin trains under Hiko for 3 years then goes to work as the Ishin faction's hit man.

As for his reasons, Kenshin believed in the ideals of the Ishin and thought that establishing a new nation ruled by the Emperor would 'bring the Japanese people happiness.' Therefore he participates in the Ishin as an assassin, killing in the name of 'justice.' However, Kenshin came to realize that killing for 'justice' is still killing, and began to feel guilt over the many lives he'd taken. This causes him much anguish for many years.

S ee Glossary
Himura Kenshin
Sagara Sanosuke
Hiko Seijuro

04 Why is Kenshin referred to as the 'Battosai'?

This word (抜刀斎) literally means 'master sword drawer', and refers to one who has mastered sword-drawing techniques. In sword-drawing, one faces the opponent with a sheathed sword, and attacks during the act of actually drawing the blade, unsheathing it so quickly and with so much force that the opponent has no time to counterattack. There are various forms of this technique, including the Iai and Nuki schools. Kenshin, who excels at quick attacks, probably used sword-drawing techniques frequently during his stint as a hit man, thus earning him the alias Battosai. Interestingly, Shishio Makoto, who replaced Kenshin as the Ishin camp's assassin, was also called the 'Battosai'. However, it seems likely that Shishio merely inherited the name with the job. Unlike Kenshin's speed, Shishio's specialty is simply cutting down his opponents and making sure they are dead, so he would probably have little use for elegant sword-drawing techniques. Although Kenshin's nickname, 'Hitokiri Battosai', became famous, no one really knew the man himself. So, when Shishio took over the job, the fact that he continued to be called the 'Battosai' perhaps indicates that the most people didn't even know about the changeover.

See Glossary

Himura Kenshin
Shishio Makoto

See questions

2 54

05 What does 'rurouni' mean? Is this Kenshin's profession?

Strictly speaking, the word 'rurouni' (流浪人) is a word created by Watsuki from the Japanese words for 'nomadism' and 'person'. One would actually expect it to be pronounced 'ruronin', but perhaps for aesthetic purposes, Watsuki dropped the final 'n' sound and writes the word るろうに..., using hiragana (Japanese phonetic characters) instead of kanji (Chinese ideographs). Simply put, the word means 'wanderer', so it does not imply any specific profession.

In particular, this word describes the many unemployable ex-samurai who remained in Japan during the Meiji period after the samurai class was abolished. During most of the Edo period, the samurai profession was highly respected. Normally each samurai belonged to a feudal domain (called a 'han'), which paid that samurai's salary. Samurai who were not employed by any domain were called ronin. Since by law there could be no samurai, not even ronin, in the Meiji period, a new word was needed to describe the directionless ex-samurai. Hence the word 'rurouni'.

⑤ee Glossary
Himura Kenshin
Meiji ishin

06 Is Kenshin based on a real person?

According to Rurouni Kenshin's author Nobuhiro Watsuki, Kenshin is based on a real assassin named Kawakami Gensai. Kawakami was one of four famous assassins of the Bakumatsu period, and was apparently so pretty he was often mistaken for a woman. Underneath his beautiful face he had nerves of steel, and is said to have been the most terrifying of the four. He was the inventor of the Furanui style, a unique form that relied on speed. He became famous when he assassinated Sakuma Shozan, a famous scholar, in broad daylight. However, not much else is known about Gensai, including whether he performed any other assassinations.

Gensai was an ardent isolationist, who advocated the expulsion of the foreigners who began entering Japan following the opening of her ports and trade relations. His opposition to the new Meiji government caused him to be arrested on fabricated charges and executed in 1871. Perhaps it was the loyalty to the principles for which Gensai, his fallen comrades, and even their enemies fought, not their actual ideology, that inspired the character of Himura Kenshin. Or maybe Watsuki was using Kenshin's character to explore an alternative history in which Gensai comes to grips with the changing times and tries to make peace with his violent past.

See Glossary
Himura Kenshin

See questions
1

About Nobuhiro Watsuki

Manga artist, born May 26, 1970. In addition to his representative work, Rurouni Kenshin, he authored Gun Blaze West (which ran in 28 installments in Shonen Jump 2001 Vol. 2 through 2001 Vol. 35) and Buso Renkin (which also ran in Shonen Jump, spanning 79 installments from 2003 Vol. 30 through 2005 Vol. 21).

He is a huge fan of the fighting game Samurai Spirits (aka Samurai Showdown) and its influence can be seen throughout Rurouni Kenshin.

Shonen Jump used to print pictures of all contributing artists on the cover of its New Year's issue, but suddenly stopped in 1998. There is a rumor that the reason Shonen discontinued the practice was that the Watsuki's photo on the 1997 issue shocked fans. According to the rumor, his actual looks were just too far removed from the images he penned for the fans to handle, and since then Shonen has stopped using photos of manga artists on its covers.

Watsuki has a detailed knowledge of Japanese history, particularly the Meiji period. Rurouni Kenshin is therefore peppered with historical events, making it a favorite among history buffs.

Prior the Meiji revolution and the establishment of the new government, it was acceptable for the Samurai caste to carry swords. Technically, Kenshin is not a samurai by birth, and shouldn't have been allowed to bear arms, but given the chaos of the period, sword ownership probably wasn't something that the crumbling Bakufu would have been able to check thoroughly. However, the Meiji government stopped recognizing the profession of samurai, and the bearing of swords was restricted to all but police and military officers. Still, the ex-samurai were very attached to their blades, and many refused to give them up. Finally, in 1876 Yamagata Aritomo (1838-1922), a military commander and politician, created a law that prohibited swords outright. This law made ownership of swords by citizens a crime (under this law, ex-samurai were considered ordinary citizens with no special status). Of course, even people like Kenshin, who had formally carried a sword as part of their job, were not entitled to an exception. The timing of the Rurouni Kenshin story arc places it 3 years after the sword ban, so we can only assume Kenshin was repeatedly hassled by the police over his weapon. It's ironic that throughout the story, Aritomo, the man who created the sword ban, should have to seek out Kenshin's help.

⑤ee Glossary
Himura Kenshin
Yamagata Aritomo

Kenshin's sword, the 'Sakabato', is odd because its cutting edge is on the wrong side, making it a seemingly useless weapon. This is of great symbolic importance to the story though. Kenshin eventually comes to regret the assassinations he committed in the past. He vows never to kill again. One would think he would then get rid of his sword altogether, but this would amount to running away from his responsibility and dishonor all those he killed in his quest to 'bring happiness to the Japanese people'. So he continues using his sword to 'bring happiness' (for example, by protecting Kaoru and others). Kenshin cannot throw away his blade while people like Shishio, whose mistaken beliefs lead him to take the lives of others, still exist.

However, having vowed never to kill again, Kenshin uses the Sakabato, a weapon that cannot cut (and therefore kill) when used normally. Being so bent on non-killing, it seems it would be better for him to carry a sword with no blade at all. However, while Kenshin avoids cutting people, he does occasionally turn the Sakabato around and use it's cutting side on objects, such as the Hishimanji Gurentai's cannon. A sword with no blade at all couldn't be used in this way to protect others.

See Glossary

Himura Kenshin
Kamiya kaoru
Sakabato

See questions

9

In the story, Arai Shakku is an exceptional swordsmith of the Bakumatsu period, famous among the Ishin supporters. He is the one who created Kenshin's Sakabato. However, when his pursuit to perfect 'well-balanced blades' turns to a single-minded obsession with perfecting 'lethal blades', the sword smith's guild shuns him. In addition to the Sakabato, he invents the Renbato, which consists of two blades stacked on top of one another so they look like a single blade. Cho of the Juppon Gatana uses this weapon. It's very difficult to treat Renbato wounds because the sword makes two cuts very close to each other. Stitching these up is very difficult, so the victim often dies. He also creates the Hakujin no Tachi, also called 'the murderer's blade'. It is a blade made of extremely thin steel, also used by Cho. The blade is so flexible that its user can conceal it by wrapping it around his/her body. It can even be curled up like a whip. Cho uses this weapon to perform his own original Orochi techniques. Shakku further shows off his twisted genius in Shishio's main weapon, the Mugenjin. The blade has a serrated edge, so that even after cutting human flesh, it doesn't lose its sharpness.

Shakku instructs his son, Seiku, in his craft, but Seiku has nothing for scorn for his father's obsession with death. In protest to his father's ways, he chooses to craft everyday cutlery, pots and pans. However Shakku, like Kenshin who once believed that killing would contribute to a brighter future, continued to create his lethal swords believing they had a role to play in creating a securer future for his son's generation. The Sakabato, the sword that cannot kill, is symbolic of Shakku's philosophy.

The Sakabato, which Kenshin first receives from Shakku is broken during a battle with Juppon Gatana member Seta Sojiro. By this time, Shakku is already dead. The only person capable of reforging it is Seiku, who is a capable swordsmith, but as mentioned, refuses to make swords. Fortunately, while still alive Shakku created two Sakabato, donating the better of the two to a Shinto shrine. Historically, Japan's swordsmiths did have a custom of making swords in pairs, one of which they kept. Kenshin receives this second Sakabato from Seiku. It is referred to as the Sakabato Shinuchi to distinguish it from its mate.

See Glossary

Himura Kenshin
Arai Shaku
Sakabato
Renbato
Hakujin no Tachi
Sawagejo Cho
Arai Seiku

See questions
8 **66**

10 What is the Hiten Mitsurugi-Ryu style?

The Hiten Mitsurugi-Ryu style, taught to Kenshin by Hiko Seijuro, is an ancient fighting style that stretches back to Japan's Sengoku period (a period of civil war that lasted from the mid-15th to until 17th century). It is optimized for one-on-many combat, and is distinguished by its speed. Kenshin's ability to read his opponents' moves and evade their attacks with split-second timing is due to his mastery of Hiten Mitsurugi-Ryu. This style has many techniques, such as the Ryusosen, Doryusen, Ryutsuisen, Hiryusen, and Ryushosen. One of the most interesting techniques is the Kuzuryusen, which uses Hiten Mitsurugi-Ryu's godlike speed to strike the target in nine places simultaneously, rendering any defense impossible. This technique was not created for actual combat, but rather as a sort of final initiation or test.

The most powerful and secret Hiten Mitsurugi-Ryu technique is the Amakakeru Ryu no Hirameki. This technique requires an iron will, and superhuman speed. Also, it cannot be mastered without taking the life of the one who teaches it. Consequently, there can only be one master of this technique living at any given time, and that person takes on the title of Hiko Seijuro and must wear the heavy, white cloak that signifies their succession to Hiten Mitsurugi-Ryu stewardship. Kenshin's instructor, Hiko Seijuro, is the 14th master.

The ideal of Hiten Mitsurugi-Ryu is to protect people from the strife of the ages. However, its power must be used neutrally, independent of any political faction. If it were used to support a particular side, that side would gain absolute authority, and the balance of power would be destroyed. Thus, for 300 years the successor of the style has had to take on the Hiko Seijuro alias -precisely so that despots couldn't use its power. However, Kenshin ignores this principle and sides with the Ishin as an assassin, causing Hiko to excommunicate him. Hiko eventually sees that Kenshin has indeed been upholding the principle of 'protecting people from strife' and teaches him the Amakakeru Ryu no Hirameki. As a result, Kenshin becomes the first Hiten Mitsurugi-Ryu master to learn the Amakakeru Ryu without killing his instructor.

See Glossary

Himura Kenshin
Hiko Seijuro
Hiten Mitsurugi-Ryu
Ryusosen
Doryusen
Ryutsuisen
Hiryusen
Ryushosen
Kuzuryusen
Amakakeru Ryu no Hirameki

See questions
37 **38** **39**

11 Why do some people say that Kenshin will never be the strongest unless he becomes the Hitokiri Battosai again?

It's said that Kenshin was the strongest swordsman in Japan while he was working as the Ishin faction's killer. Normally, killing is something that sane people are hesitant about doing, so Kenshin must have had to put himself into a pretty ruthless mindset and almost forget himself entirely in order to kill in cold blood. In a sense, he was a schizophrenic, slipping into a completely separate persona -the Hitokiri Battosai- while working. Currently, Kenshin continues to fight, but has vowed never to kill. Compared to his former self, he no longer has the ruthless killer-instinct that made him such a feared opponent. For this reason, Jin-e and Saito attempt to provoke him into reverting to his Hitokiri Battosai persona.

See Glossary
Himura Kenshin

See questions
2 4

12 What's the Achilles' heel of the Hiten Mitsurugi-Ryu's Amakakeru Ryu no Hirameki technique?

The Amakakeru Ryu no Hirameki is a sword-drawing technique that uses super-human speed to attack the opponent before he/she has time to land a blow. To make this possible, a unique stance is used. In sword-drawing, one normally steps forward with the right foot to avoid cutting ones' own leg off. However, when Kenshin uses the Amakakeru Ryu no Hirameki, he steps out with his left foot. It is this split-second difference in speed and force that separates normal sword-drawing from the Amakakeru Ryu no Hirameki technique. The Achilles' heel is that the unusual stance lets the opponent know that it's coming. However, even with knowledge of this weakness, the Amakakeru Ryu no Hirameki is so devastatingly fast that only someone with truly legendary sword skills could defend against it.

See questions
10

Kenshin has a distinctive cross-shaped scar on the left side of his face. According to Megumi, the scar itself is superficial and should have healed long ago. Its reason for remaining must be psychological. Indeed, the scar does represent a deep psychological trauma for Kenshin. He got the scar about a year after beginning his career as an assassin. He didn't get both halves of the 'x' at the same time though. A young man named Kiyosato Akira gives Kenshin the longer of the scars when he's sent to kill Shigekura Jubei, the man Kiyosato is guarding.

Kenshin kills Kiyosato, and his fiancé named Tomoe, vows revenge. She becomes a spy, which allows her to eventually live with Kenshin. However, Tomoe ends up falling in love with her target. The feeling is mutual, and they wed. As a result, Tomoe ends up betraying the Yaminobu (the group of spies she belonged to), but it seems this was part of their plan. The Yaminobu had foreseen that Tomoe might fall in love with Kenshin, and had planned on using that to their advantage. In the final battle with the Yaminobu, Kenshin is struck deaf and blind by their attack and ends up killing Tomoe trying to defend himself. It is at this time that Tomoe gives Kenshin the second part of the scar with the knife she's carrying. Naturally Kenshin feels guilt over killing his own wife, and his misery only increases when he reads Tomoe's diary and learns that she was Kiyosato's fiancé. The double impact of learning that he robbed Tomoe of happiness by killing her future husband, then killed her with his own hands, created two deep psychological scars, which are reflected in the two physical scars on his face.

See Glossary
Himura Kenshin
Takani Megumi
Kiyosato Akira

See Glossary
Koenma
Urameshi Yusuke
Yukimura Keiko
Kuwabara kazuma
Botan

14 How does Kenshin make a living?

About 10 years have passed since Kenshin became an unemployed drifter and began wandering Japan. After taking up residence in Kaoru's dojo, we never really see him engaged in any employment. As one of the central Ishin supporters who helped bring the new rulers to power, he is in a position to receive a relatively high post in the Meiji government, but he turns down every offer that comes his way. Indeed, Yamagata Aritomo, former commander of the Ishin Kiheitai army (one of the strongest forces of the revolution) and leader of the Meiji government's armed forces, worries about Kenshin and spends many years searching for him. Kenshin turns even Yamagata's offer down in the end.

This means Kenshin is virtually unemployed, so how does he make a living? Does he just mooch off of Kaoru? Given his personality, this seems unlikely. It's possible that he collected some form of minimum living stipend from the Meiji government. Or, with the end of the revolution, perhaps he was entitled to some sort of 'retirement' pension as his services were no longer required.

See Glossary
Himura Kenshin
Kamiya Kaoru
Yamagata Aritomo

See questions
2 25

Name: **Sagara Sanosuke**
Occupation: **Fighter-for-hire**

Leaving home at the age of 9, Sanosuke joins the Sekihotai, whose captain, Sagara Sozo, Sanosuke idolizes as a mentor. Unfortunately, the Sekihotai is accused of impersonating the government army, and Sozo is sentenced to death. Sanosuke eventually moves to Tokyo, where he operates as a fighter-for-hire under the alias of Zanza, a name that soon becomes famous in the city's underground circles. He becomes quite arrogant and arbitrary, charging clients based on how "fun" the fights are. His opponents are often so traumatized by their encounter with him that they see his trademark à´ (aku bad, evil) ideograph in their dreams for months afterwards. Sanosuke initially harbors great bitterness towards the new Meiji government due to the execution of his mentor Sagara, but joins forces with Kenshin after being beaten by him. An incredibly resilient fighter, Sanosuke gives even Kenshin (who usually can defeat opponents with a single blow) a run for his money.

相楽左之助

15 How much is known about Sanosuke's personal history?

When Kenshin first meets him, Sanosuke is still the brawler known as Zanza. At that time it's learned that Sanosuke left home at the age of 9 to join the Sekihotai. He idolized the captain, Sagara Sozo, as a mentor and even took on Sagara's family name as his own. Other than this, not much is said about Sanosuke's background. However, in the latter half of the story, we learn that Sanosuke's real name is Higashidani, son of Kamishimoemon, a humble radish farmer. His mother, Naname, has passed away. It's also revealed that he has a younger sister, Uki, and a little brother, Ota. Kamishimoemon is big-hearted but bellicose, so it's easy to see where Sanosuke gets his personality.

See Glossary

Himura Kenshin
Sagara Sanosuke
Sagara Sozo
Higashidani Kamishimoemon
Higashidani Nanamae
Hidashidani Uki

See questions
17

See Glossary

Urameshi Yusuke
Urameshi Atsuko
Yukimura Keiko

16 Is it true that Sanosuke is based on a real person?

See Glossary

Sagara Sanosuke
Shinsengumi
Zanbato

It's said that Watsuki, Rurouni Kenshin's creator, modeled Sanosuke on Harada Sanosuke, a real person and the captain of the 10th squad of Shinsengumi. Harada Sanosuke was said to be exceptionally handsome and skilled at using spears. He was a determined soldier, participating in all the major battles fought by the Shinsengumi. He had a violent, extremely impatient personality, but it's also said that he was a bit fragile, perhaps due to insecurity over his middling rank. He cherished his comrades and looked after those under his command with great care. He also is said to have been almost childlike in his habit of judging things in black and white terms. It seems that Watsuki incorporated a lot of these traits into Sanosuke's character.

Historically, it's recorded that Harada Sanosuke died during the Ueno War, but one legend says he escaped to the continent and became a bandit king. This seems to be the inspiration for the ending of Rurouni Kenshin, which has Sanosuke crossing over to the continent. Sanosuke's peculiar weapon, the Zanbato, also might have been inspired by Harada's preference for the spear, an unusual weapon for the Shinsengumi, which favored swords.

T he Sekihotai was an actual organization. It was composed of private citizens and established in 1868, directly after the battle of Toba-Fushima. As the Ishin army marched towards Edo, the Sekihotai would move ahead, probing the various provinces and trying to increase support for them, as they sort of served as scouts. Their leader was a man named Sagara Sozo. He lead the 1st corps of the Sekihotai, and was in charge of propagandizing the imperialists' promise to halve land taxes (implying that supporting the Ishin would lead to a halving of taxes). Later finances became tight and the new government, unable to keep its promise to lower taxes, accused the 1st corps of the Sekihotai with impersonating a government army, and had Sagara Sozo beheaded.

In Rurouni Kenshin, Sagara Sozo is very cool, but the actual man was more dynamic. His real name was Kojima Shiro, and he was originally not a warrior, having been born into a local administrative family. He dreamed of founding a new gov-

See Glossary

Sarayashiki Public Junior High School
Urameshi Yusuke
Kuwabara Kazuma
Yukimura Keiko
Akashi
Iwamoto
Okubo

ernment, and left his home and friends to become an active patriot during the chaotic times of the Meiji upheaval. His story is a tragic one, ending in his disgracing and execution at age 29. His tale seems to have touched the history-loving Watsuki deeply, which might explain Sanosuke's decision to adopt Sagara Sozo's family name.

See Glossary

Sagara Sanosuke
Sagara Sozo

See questions

15

18 What sort of weapon is Sanosuke's Zanbato

This extremely large, heavy weapon was reportedly used in Japan during the 16th century (Azuchi-Momoyama period). Its main purpose was to bring down warhorses. Though, it was not used very often. Partly because warhorses were valuable and it was a wiser strategy to dismount the rider and capture the horse. Its size and weight also made it unlikely that many people could have used it effectively. An unusual weapon indeed, which is probably why it was selected to represent the dynamism of Sanosuke, who himself is modeled on the spear-wielding Harada. However, perhaps realizing that Sanosuke's extreme resiliency and power are best displayed in hand-to-hand combat, the Zanbato's role plays little after Sanosuke's battle with Kenshin. Sanosuke's nickname, "Zanza", derived from Zanbato, also disappears from the story.

See Glossary
Sagara Sanosuke
Zanbato

See questions
16

19 What is the "Futae no Kiwami" technique that Sanosuke learns to use?

Sanosuke learns the "Futae no Kiwami" from Yukyuzan Anji, originally an adversary from the Juppon Gatana. Anji, a former Buddhist monk, develops this technique in the course of his quest for "salvation". In a normal punch, the fist meets physical resistance from the target. However, at the moment of impact, the target's resistance and the force of the punch cancel each other out, leaving the target with zero resistance. If a second punch is landed at this moment of zero resistance, an incredibly powerful blow can be delivered, as the target will have no resistance. If executed correctly, this technique can smash stones into dust. However, it's nearly impossible to master, and even Anji, its inventor, struggled with it for 10 years. Sanosuke learned the technique from Anji under the condition that Anji would kill him if he couldn't master it in one week. It's a testament to his talent that Sanosuke succeeds in learning the technique in this short time. After Saito Hajime's observation that Sanosuke's defense is weak, Sanosuke insightfully

S ee Glossary

Sagara Sanosuke
Futae no Kiwami
Yukyuzan Anji
Juppon Gatana

See questions
63

decides to focus on offense, realizing that it suits him better. There was also a lot of luck involved, as Sanosuke happened to be on his way to Kyoto at the time, and just bumped into Anji, who taught him the "Futae no Kiwami".

20 Sanosuke seems virtually indestructible. What's his secret?

Everyone who fights Sanosuke is shocked at how much punishment he can take. It may be genetic, since his father, Kamishimoemon, is also an adept brawler who seems to shrug off punches. Another part of it could be Sanosuke's diet. After every meal, he can be seen chewing on a fish bone. In fact, he eats a lot of fish, and even orders salmon at Akabeko, which specializes in beef dishes. His healthy diet of fish and the superhuman amounts of calcium he absorbs from all those fish bones, may have combined to give him a heavy-duty skeleton.

See Glossary

Sagara Sanosuke
Akabeko

21 | What's the deal with Sanosuke's nickname obsession?

Although himself labeled a "bird-head" by Hiruma Gohei, Sanosuke seems to love branding others with bizarre nicknames. In particular, he's good at accurately pigeon-holing his victims. He seems to have a quick mind when it comes to personal abuse. A few examples follow.

Hiruma Kihei, "Anti-Ebisu": Ebisu, deity of wealth and commerce, is known for his jolly smile. This nickname comes from the forced affability with which Kihei first approaches the Kamiya Dojo.

Hiruma Gohei, "Meat Daruma": A Daruma is an egg-shaped Japanese doll with no arms or legs.This nickname implies that Gohei is just a useless lump of muscles.

Takani Megumi, "Fox Lady": Megumi's appearance seems to have reminded Sanosuke of a fox. In Japanese legends, female foxes are said to deceive humans. Following along these lines, he takes to calling Kaoru "Tanuki Girl" and Misao "Weasel Girl".

Shikijo "Meaty Moron" or "Patchwork Daruma": The first name ridicules Shikijo for relying on his strength alone. The second comes from Shikijo's scar-covered body.

Isurgi Raijuta "The Old Shuttlecock": Derived from Raijuta's costume.

Saito Hajime "Micro-eyed Jerk": From the fact that Saito has narrow eyes.

These examples illustrate Sanosuke's penchant for coming up with dead-on nicknames based on his victim's appearance.

22 Is Sanosuke in love with Megumi?

Sanosuke initially regards Megumi as an enemy, since she made the opium that killed one of his friends. He also gives her the rather unflattering name "Fox Lady". However, he gradually comes to rely on her medical skills, and when his right hand is injured, he goes straight to her. Sanosuke is usually loath to show weakness in front of others or rely on their help, but in the case of Megumi he makes an exception. He seems to feel that he can let his guard down with her. This isn't to say that he loves her romantically. Rather, he probably sees her as an older-sister figure who he can count on. Given Sanosuke's personality, in all likelihood he would try to act even more manly around a girl he was in love with. If he loved Megumi, he would probably act as a tough-guy, and not ask her to tend to his wounds. For her part, Megumi also appears to look after Sanosuke like a little brother. These two, while always swapping insults, are pretty much on the same wavelength.

See Glossary
Sagara Sanosuke
Takani Megumi

See questions
21

Name: **Kamiya kaoru**
Occupation: **Kamiya Kasshin-ryu instructor.**

Koaru's father, Kamiya Koshijiro abhorred using swords for killing, and sought instead to use them to bring out the potential in people. However, as a member of the police battotai (sword unit), he was called up to serve in the Seinan war, where he lost his life. Kaoru now keeps the Kamiya Dojo running herself. During the imposter Battosai incident, she loses her students, but later gets the dojo on back on its feet with Kenshin as a lodger and Yahiko as a student. Kaoru is famous for her terrible cooking

神谷 薫

23 How is Kaoru as a swordswoman?

At the young age of 17, Kaoru is already an instructor in Kamiya Kasshin-ryu, so her abilities must be quite high. Even after her father dies, she continues to instruct 10 students until the imposter Battosai incident, and even after she loses her students to the machinations of Kihei and Gohei, she continues to teach young swordsmen at the nearby Chuetsuryu Maekawa Dojo. She's extremely popular, and whenever she gives a class there, 3 times the normal number of students show up. Yahiko also improves conspicuously once he starts taking daily lessons from Kaoru, illustrating her teaching abilities, which means her fencing skills must be impeccable.

Koshijiro must have been very rigorous with Kaoru's training, so that she could someday succeed him in running the dojo. The fact that Kaoru is so inept at cooking and housework is also probably a side effect of her almost exclusive focus on her training. When she falls in love with Kenshin, who has many enemies, she trains all the harder to become stronger, not wanting to slow him down.

See Glossary
Kamiya Kaoru
Kamiya Kasshin-Ryu
Hiruma Kihei
Hiruma Gohei
Maekawa Miyauchi
Myojin Yahiko
Kamiya Koshijiro

24 Can Kaoru's cooking really be that bad?

Whenever Kaoru cooks for the gang, she's invariably subjected to a fusillade of taunts. One can't help feel sorry for her. Sanosuke repeatedly and frankly tells Kaoru her cooking stinks, and suggests that he teach her how to cook. This seems quite cheeky considering she's always feeding him for free. Further, even the kindly Kenshin damns her with faint praise, calling her cooking a delicacy...of a sort. When Megumi brings over some handmade sweets, everyone sings her praises, while noting that in comparison, Kaoru's sweets are like 'mud balls'. Worse still, when Megumi tries Kaoru's cooking, she blurts out "Ugh! It's awful!" It's probably safe to assume that Kaoru's father raised her to be a swordswoman, not a housewife, and as a result she never really learned to cook. Even so, does she really deserve all the abuse she receives?

Actually, only Yahiko doesn't complain (much). He is a growing boy, so he'll probably eat just about anything with gusto. Still, considering that

See Glossary

Kamiya Kaoru
Sagara Sanosuke
Himura Kenshin
Tanani Megumi
Myojin Yahiko

he loves insulting Kaoru, the fact that he doesn't mock her cooking probably means that it isn't all that bad. Also, although everyone complains, they always clean their plates. In the case of Sanosuke and Megumi, they're always taunting Kaoru anyway, so their critiques are suspect. They both have abrasive personalities, so it would be out of character for them to offer praise. It's more likely that since they're all good friends, they can get away with the abuse. In Kenshin's case, this is probably the only thing he can tease Kaoru about, but the effect of his ribbing is exaggerated when combined with that of Sanosuke and Megumi. So, we can conclude that while Kaoru's cooking isn't great, it's not as bad as everyone says.

After all the Kamiya Dojo's students quit during the imposter Battosai incident, Yahiko is the only pupil. Although Kaoru is committed to spreading her father's ideal of using fencing to bring out the potential in people rather than for killing, she never gets any new students.

Whenever Kaoru teaches at the Maekawa Dojo, 3 times the normal number of students show up. The Maekawa Dojo even enjoys a spike in membership because a lot of students specifically want to take lessons from Kaoru. One wonders why they don't just enroll in Kaoru's dojo directly. Kaoru certainly wants new students desperately. After Kenshin publicly trounces the Police Swordmen, a number of students visit the Kamiya Dojo to inquire about training. However, they leave when Kenshin explains that he's not the one who'd be teaching them. Angry, Kaoru smacks Kenshin with a shinai for letting the potential pupils go.

One explanation for the lack of students is that the Kamiya Dojo has a whiff of danger about it.

See Glossary

Kamiya Kaoru
Myojin Yahiko
Maekawa MIyauchi
Himura Kenshin

See questions
23

Because Kenshin lives there, the dojo is constantly in trouble, and has been attacked repeatedly. As a result, it's probably a place the townsfolk stay away from.

26 Is it true that Kaoru has an artistic side?

When Kenshin takes on the mission of eliminating Shishio, he goes to Kyoto alone, not wanting to endanger Kaoru and his friends. This doesn't stop them though and Kaoru & co. go to Kyoto to look for him. As part of their search for Kenshin, they post a sketch of him at Shirobeko. The likeness, drawn by Kaoru, is so good, it has lead to speculation among Japanese Rurouni Kenshin fans as to Kaoru's artistic talents. Of course, while Kaoru draws the portrait in the story, like all the other images in the series, it is actually drawn by Watsuki, so its unsurprising that the likeness is spot on. However, in one episode we learn that Kaoru's grandfather was an artist. In the imposter Battosai incident, Kaoru loses her students and sells one of her grandfather's paintings to make ends meet. It's not impossible then that she inherited some of this artistic talent.

See Glossary
Kamiya Kaoru
Himura Kenahin
Shishio Makoto
Shirobeko

27 Kaoru and Megumi don't seem to get along very well. Are they on bad terms?

Kaoru and Megumi seem to argue whenever they meet. The source of their tiffs is often rivalry over Kenshin, but in fact they're not really enemies. Megumi knows that Kaoru has a quick temper, and more often than not is intentionally pushing her buttons for fun. Megumi is also much older than Kaoru, and likes to lord her seniority over her. On the other hand, Kaoru is openly hostile to Megumi, who often makes overtly amorous advances towards Kenshin, and perceives her as a rival.

For her part, Megumi seems to think of Kaoru like a little sister. While Megumi does seem to love Kenshin (and being an adult she refuses to hide this), she recognizes that Kaoru is a better match for Kenshin than herself. Far from resenting Kaoru, Megumi is actually doing her best to stay out of her way. However, Megumi will lecherously glom onto Kenshin as a roundabout way of spurring on Kaoru when she gets too complacent in the relationship (or maybe Megumi just can't keep her hands off him). The main difference between the two is that at 22, Megumi is a bit more laid back, while the 17 year-old Kaoru takes

See Glossary
Kamiya Kaoru
Takani Megumi
Himura Kenshin

51

everything at face value. So, though Megumi puts the moves on Kenshin as a way of motivating Kaoru, Kaoru doesn't understand this until Megumi actually gives her direct encouragement. Eventually Kaoru comes to appreciate the thought behind Megumi's actions. The two actually have very similar personalities, and essentially get along very well.

The Rurouni Kenshin

Companion

Minor Character's Secrets

Rurouni Kenshin Profile 004

Name: Myojin Yahiko

Occupation: Kamiya Kasshin-Ryu pupil, and helper at Akabeko

Born into a Tokyo family descended from samurai. His father was poor to begin with, but with the beginning of the Meiji era the samurai's traditional rank was abolished, causing the family to slide even deeper into poverty. His father was killed fighting the government army in the Ueno War. His mother died of illness brought on by overwork. With no relatives left, Yahiko was forced to work as a pickpocket for the Yakuza for awhile, but is rescued by Kenshin and moves into the Kamiya Dojo as a student.

明神弥彦

Rurouni Kenshin is set in Japan's Meiji period. Preceding this was the Edo period, a time in which samurai were central to society. During this period, there was a caste system composed of four classes: samurai, farmer, artisan, and merchant. Yahiko's family was originally samurai, the highest class. However, before Yahiko was born, the Meiji period ushered in a new system of government, and the samurai were abolished.

So, although Yahiko comes from a good family and was probably raised well, in Meiji Japan he is just an ordinary citizen. The yakuza who force Yahiko into thievery advise him to forget his samurai ancestry; the modern world, they say, has no place for the pride of the samurai, and those who cling to it just fall into ruin. In a sense, they are correct in that the former-samurai who stuck to the old traditions during the Meiji period were unable to grasp the realities of the new era and often fell behind the times.

Still, holding onto one's pride is not always a bad

S ee Glossary
Myojin Yahiko

55

thing. It is his samurai pride that leads Yahiko to decide to stop stealing. One way of looking at Yahiko's character is that he was created to illustrate the tragedies caused by that era's upheaval.

Yahiko's desire to become a strong swordsman drives him to practice day and night as a student of the Kamiya Kasshin style under Kaoru. Although frustrated by his own apparent lack of progress, with Kaoru's guidance he actually improves steadily without realizing it. When he fights the Nagaoka Mikio gang to help Tsubame, he surprises even himself with his ability to read his opponents' moves.

This is probably in part due to Kaoru's excellent training, and also to his own natural abilities. He learns to perform Kenshin's Hiten Mitsurugiri Ryu technique just by watching, and uses the secret Kamiya Kasshin techniques Mamorihadome, and Semehawatari, which he's just mastered, to create a new offensive technique in actual battle. Even compared to the other "naturals", such as Kenshin, who became active as the "Hitokiri Battosai" at 14, and Shinomori Aoshi, who became the head of the Edo Oniwabanshu at 15, Yahiko's mastery of the Kamiya Kasshin-Ryu's secrets at age 10 shows he has a fair amount of natural talent.

See Glossary
Myojin Yahiko
Mamiya Kasshin-Ryu
Nagaoka Mikio
Hiten Mitsurugi-Ryu
Mamorihadome
Semehawatari
Shinomori Aoshi
Oniwabaushu

Name: **Takani Megumi**
Occupation: **Assistant doctor.**

高荷恵

Daughter of Takani Ryusei, a doctor from the Aizu province. Her family is scattered during the Aizu War. After this, she travels to Tokyo and begins assisting a certain doctor, 5 years before the story arc. This doctor manufactures "Spider's Web" opium with Takeda Kanryu, but Takeda kills him 3 years before the story opens. Megumi is confined by Kanryu and forced to produced opium, but is later freed by Kenshin and company. She then begins working at Gensai-sensei's clinic.

30 | What sort of man was Takani Ryusei?

The Takani family is famous for producing generations of doctors. It also appears to be quite a progressive family for the time, as medicine is taught to the women and children too. Megumi's father was widely known for providing equal care to all patients. Give the rigid class divisions of the Edo period, it appears that those of the warrior class looked down on Takani for giving his full attention to any patients regardless of their caste. Nonetheless, among other medical practitioners he was highly respected and called an ideal doctor.

While Takani understood the benefits of rangaku (Western medicine), its study was forbidden in Aizu province. So, he moved his entire household to Nagasaki. In those days, leaving one's native province was an undertaking requiring quite a bit of resolve, but Takani was a man of ideals and action. Later, about the time he's permitted to re-enter Aizu, the Edo period ends in the Meiji Ishin, and Takani is killed in the Aizu War, one of the decisive Boshin Wars.

See Glossary
Takani Megumi
Meiji Ishin

31 What's the story behind the war that separates Megumi from her family?

The Aizu War was a war between Japan's Ishin government army and the province of Aizu. Aizu continued to recognize the authority of the shogun, and was therefore considered rebellious. In contrast to the overwhelming might of the government army, Aizu sent out men and women of all ages to fight. Aizu resisted, but was eventually defeated by the government's modern weapons on September 22, 1868.

Before the Ishin, Aizu had the job of policing Kyoto, housed a contingent of Shinsengumi and sometimes cracked down on the Ishin activists. Consequently, after their defeat the people of Aizu were subject to a long period of discrimination by the government.

See Glossary
Takani Megumi
Meiji Ishin

See questions
32

32 Why does Megumi cooperate with Kanryu's opium cartel?

The Aizu War results in the death of Megumi's father and the scattering of her family. Alone, Megumi travels to the capital and begins working for a doctor. It's possible that she thought that building connections with doctors would improve her chances of finding her family again.

Unfortunately the doctor who employs her turns out to be working with Kanryu in an opium venture. This doctor develops the new "Spider's Web" opium, which uses special refinement techniques to produce very potent opium that is twice as addictive as normal opium, but only uses half the raw opium. Megumi is an unwittingly accomplice in the refinement of "Spider's Web".

In a short time of its release, "Spider's Web" opium catches on in Tokyo. Seeing the potential for profit, Kanryu plans to mass market the drug, and asks the doctor to show him the refinement process. The doctor, wishing to monopolize the profits himself, refuses to give up the recipe, and so Kanryu kills him. This leaves Megumi as the only person who understands the refinement process. Kanryu imprisons her, and forces her to produce opium for him.

S ee Glossary
Takani Megumi
Takeda Kanryu

See questions
31

61

Incidentally, opium has a long history of medicinal use. During the 19th century, the era in which Rurouni Kenshin is set, oral use of laudanum was acceptable in Europe. So, given Megumi's medical background, perhaps the doctor told her she was making "medicinal use" opium, and she didn't realize the drug was actually being used unethically for profit. However, in Japan opium use was strictly forbidden during that period. Those selling it or trying to entice others to try it were executed. So maybe Megumi was acting out of despair and a subliminal desire to die.

The Origins of the Samurai

There are a number of competing theories on the origins of the samurai. Previously, the most accepted theory was that sometime during the Heian period, when Japan was still ruled by the Imperial Family and aristocracy, powerful local agricultural families took up arms to protect themselves from brigands. This was the origin of the bushi or warrior caste.

Meanwhile, the aristocracy, which was extremely pacifist, had disbanded their armies. This created a minor problem as the aristocracy found themselves unprotected, necessitating the employment of said bushi as bodyguards. These bodyguards were referred to as saburau, which means to "attend or serve by one's side". Over time, this word saburau eventually morphed into the word samurai. In modern Japanese, samurai and bushi are used interchangeably, but technically the samurai is the higher ranked of the two.

Eventually, these bushi and samurai became strong enough to rebel. The aristocracy, with no army and faced by a rebellion comprised of their own bodyguards, could not hope to put down the rebels. The result of this weakening of Japan's central power was that "bushi groups" appeared in all areas of Japan and attempted to seize power, ending in the emergence of Yoritomo Minamoto as Japan's new ruler. His political system came to be called the bakufu. From then on, other samurai repeatedly staged coup d'etat. The story of Rurouni Kenshin picks up at the end of this process during the Meiji Ishin. During this time, a struggle was underway to topple the Edo Bakufu (founded by a samurai named Tokugawa Ieyasu), ostensibly to restore the Emperor as Japan's ruler.

Name: **Hajime Saito**

Occupation: **Assistant Inspector, Metropolitan Police**

Originally the leader of the 3rd squad of the Shinsengumi. Following the Ishin, he changes his name to Fujita Goro and becomes Assistant Inspector by way of serving as a police swordsman during the Seinan War. He is an expert in Gatotsu, a technique in which thrusts, rather than slashes, are used.

Saito Hajime (1844-1915) was indeed a real person, but as his role in Rurouni Kenshin is fairly important to the story, the artist has taken a lot of creative license. While the real Saito is described as something of a dandy and a "carpet knight", in Rurouni Kenshin he's rather more villainous. Saito did in fact originally serve in the Shinsengumi, and then became an Assistant Inspector in the Metropolitan Police after the Ishin. However, in contrast to the Rurouni Kenshin version of Saito, who doesn't touch alcohol because it "makes him want to kill people", the real Saito loved booze. Historical mistakes such as these have apparently led to some complaints from Ishin buffs.

斉藤一

During the end of the Edo period, Japan was divided between those in favor of keeping the existing Bakufu, and those who advocated moving to a form of government centered on the Emperor. Organized by Aizu province, the Shinsengumi supported the Bakufu and were charged with keeping the peace in Kyoto, which was frequently rocked by internal violence.

In the Rurouni Kenshin universe, this makes them rivals of Kenshin during his pro-revolutionary activities. The Shinsengumi were also called "the wolves of Mibu", since they were first organized in the Mibu region. They were recognizable by their pale yellow or blue, red and white striped haori and their flag, which simply bore the ideograph "誠" (truth, sincerity, or fidelity) in red.

They were all excellent swordsman who fought fearlessly to protect Kyoto, but were ultimately destroyed by the Ishin faction's modern weapons. They were perhaps the last and strongest of Japan's swordsmen, and they have continued to play an

See Glossary
Sito Hajime
Shinsengumi

active role in stories ever since. Indeed, the Shinsengumi still enjoy popularity, inspiring novels, movies and hit TV series. Interestingly, Saito's signature thrusting (Gatotsu) technique was originally developed as a group attack for use against individual opponents. It was created by Hijikata Toshizo, the much praised second in command of the Shinsengumi, as a more efficient method of eliminating enemies.

See Glossary
Gatotsu
Hijikata Toshizo

As an alumnus of the Shinsengumi, which excelled at efficiently disposing of enemies, Saito picks the most effective form of Gatotsu depending on the strength of his enemy. Thus, he uses less powerful attacks for weaker enemies, and more powerful attacks for stronger opponents. There are a numer of variations of Gatotsu, as listed below.

Gatotsu Ishiki: his standard, most conservative attack.

Gatotsu Nishiki: strong downward thrust, for use when he has the high ground.

Gatotsu Sanshiki: upward thrust, for use when his opponent has the high ground.

Gatotsu Zeroshiki: close range technique, using thrusts delivered with the upper-body only.

See Glossary
Saito Hajime
Shinsengumi
Gatotsu

Name: **Kyoto Oniwabanshu**
Occupation: **Spies**

京都御庭番衆

The Oniwabanshu were originally organized in the Edo period to protect Edo Castle (where the Tokugawa Shogun resided). In Rurouni Kenshin, with the arrival of Perry's "Black Ships", Japan's sovereignty is called into question. The Kyoto Oniwabanshu are a group of spies the Shogun sends to Kyoto, suspecting the Emperor and court nobles are becoming deeply involved in politics. The Oniwabanshu are based in a restaurant, the Aoiya, and consist of Kashiwazaki Kinen (a.k.a. Okina), Kuro, Shiro, Omasu, Okon, and Misao. Staying in Edo are the "Onmitsu Oniwabanshu" led by Shinomori Aoshi. While the latter are fierce rivals of Kenshin's group, the former actually help Kenshin and become his allies.

35 Is Kashiwazaki Nenji any good as a warrior?

Okina seems nothing more than a selfish, lecherous old man, but during the closing days of the Edo period, his savvy put him within reach of leading the Oniwabanshu. In the end however, Aoshi was given that honor. Okina specializes in Chinese kenpo using tonfan. Although he loses in a fight with Aoshi, his own pupil, this might be due to his age more than anything else. In his younger days, he might have been as strong as or stronger than Aoshi.

See Glossary
Oniwabanshu
Shinomori Aoshi

36 What sort of weapons are Misao's Kansatsu Tobikunai?

Misao specializes in the use of Kansatsu Tobikunai, or small throwing knives. She can throw several at a time, dealing serious damage to her enemies. These weapons fall under the same category as the shuriken, made famous by the ninja, and in fact some ninja actually used a weapon very similar to Misao's Tobikunai.

Because the knives are light, they're well suited to Misao, who's a rather petite girl. They can be used to attack from a distance or from cover, making them handy for sneak attacks. Misao's costume, ability to take advantage of her light frame, and affinity for missile weapons, suggest strongly that her character is patterned on the ninja mold. The other members of the Kyoto Oniwabanshu also seem to use ninjutsu techniques, such as Omasu's (Masukami) circular shuriken, Okon's (Omime) Hakunoji shuriken, and the Koteha shuriken of Kurojo and Hakujo.

See Glossary

Makimachi Misao
Kansatsu Tobikunai
Omasu
Okon
Kurojo
Hakujo

The pros and cons of Japan's seclusion policy

Until Commodore Perry forced Japan to open its ports in 1853, Japan had followed a seclusion policy which restricted contact with other countries.

One of the motivations for this policy was stopping the propagation of Christianity by foreign missionaries. It was thought that Christianity was destabilizing to public order, and that its converts would stop obeying the bakufu.

A further motivation could have been preventing Japan's silver from leaving the country. At the time, Japan was a prominent silver producer, and silver was often required for transactions of silk and other commodities with foreign countries. Because the government could not control all foreign transactions, large amounts of silver left the country. Thus, the bakufu government limited foreign trade to a few countries.

A third reason may have had to do with public order. Rather than prepare for military adventures abroad, the government thought it better to focus their forces on maintaining public order domestically. The seclusion policy may have been used to remove the possibility of military competition with foreign powers from the equation.

During its long seclusion, Japan did fall behind the rest of the Western world's technological advancements. On the other hand, a unique domestic culture flourished during this period.

Name: **Seijuro Hiko**
Occupation: **13th successor of the Hiten Mitsurugi-Ryu style**

Currently works as a potter under the name Niitsuka Kunoshin. His ego is enormous, but his mastery of Hiten Mitsurugi-Ryu probably justifies it.

比古清十郎

37 Is Hiko Seijuro's real name known?

See Glossary
Hiko Seijuro
Hiten Mitsurugi-Ryu
Himura Kenshin

See questions
10

Kenshin's master is known by the name Hiko Seijuro, but this is more of a title that is conferred on successors of the Hiten Mitsurugi-Ryu style, not his real name. Warriors who use Hiten Mitsurugi-Ryu are very strong, and the official successor of the style is said to be practically invincible. If such a person were to become involved in, for example, politics, the authority of whatever side he/she supported would become absolute.

Consequently, Hiten Mitsurugi-Ryu successors are forbidden from participating in politics, as they are too powerful. They must keep their distance from such matters, hide their true character, and use the title of Hiko Seijuro in place of their true name. Hiko Seijuro has further distanced himself from the world by secluding himself in the mountains and posing as a potter by the name of Niitsuka Kunoshin. This is likely not his real name either. In fact, his true name is never revealed in the series. It is left a mystery.

The white cloak that Hiko Seijuro always wears is an ongoing tradition of the masters of Hiten Mitsurugi-Ryu, like the title "Hiko Seijuro". As there can be only one master at any given time, the cloak is taken along with the life of the previous wearer. In other words, it proves that the wearer is the only person who can wield all of the Hiten Mitsurugi-Ryu's techniques. There is a secret within the cloak itself too. The cloak is very heavy, and just wearing it is a burden. It has the dual purpose of restraining the Hiten Mitsurugi-Ryu successors, keeping their formidable power in check, while simultaneously making them even stronger. Kenshin, having mastered all the Hiten Mitsurugi-Ryu techniques, would normally have to wear this cloak and change his name to Hiko Seijuro. However, he decides the cloak doesn't suit him, and more importantly, he is the first person in the history of Hiten Mitsurugi-Ryu to succeed in mastering its secrets without killing his predecessor. So it comes to pass that Hiten Mitsurugi-Ryu ends up with two masters, and Hiko Seijuro keeps the cloak.

On the other hand, the Spirit World probably judged that not having a physical body would prove a hindrance to investigating demons in the human world. Therefore, when she becomes a detective's assistant, she comes to the human world in a human body. Thus, even people like Keiko, who don't have a sixth sense per se, can see her.

See Glossary
Hiko Seijuro
Hiten Mitsurugi-Ryu

See questions
37

We're told that Kenshin's master, Hiko Seijuro, is 43, but he looks nowhere near that old. Kenshin also looks much younger than his 28 years, and everyone who meets him is astonished to hear his true age. The secret to their youthfulness must have to do with Hiten Mitsurugi-Ryu. Its techniques are characterized by speed. Practitioners must learn to move and attack faster than normal humans. Perhaps the continuous training puts the body in a constant state of readiness, which protects the cells from aging. In any case, it is unlikely that Kenshin and Hiko Seijuro both just happen to be genetically gifted with a youthful appearance Judgment is not Lord Yama, but Koenma! Perhaps Lord Yama takes frequent vacations?

See Glossary
Hiko Seijuro
Hiten Mitsurugi-Ryu
Himura Kenshin

40 Why does Hiko Seijuro play such a brief role in the story?

Aside from Kenshin's training scenes, Hiko only really appears during the battle with Fuji, the giant from the Juppon Gatana gang. There's actually an inside story about Hiko's absence from the story.

In a nutshell, the Rurouni Kenshin universe revolves around the question of how Kenshin will confront and defeat his powerful rivals. This is a favorite running theme of Shonen Jump, the magazine that carried Rurouni Kenshin. Jump's editors apparently required that Watsuki develop the story accordingly. Following this concept to its logical conclusion, if Kenshin were to be defeated, the story would end, because it hinges on confirming and reconfirming that Kenshin is indeed the strongest.

However, if Hiko Seijuro (who's even stronger than Kenshin) played a major part in the story, it wouldn't really matter who Kenshin fought. Hiko would be a sort of ultimate trump card, leaving no suspense in the battles. Therefore, the editors asked Watsuki not to include Hiko very often, and consequently his role is kept small. As the Hiten Mitsurugi-Ryu's teachings imply, this style's matters are too powerful to be allowed to side with any particular cause. They must be kept neutral and far removed from worldly matters to avoid upsetting the power-balance.

See Glossary

Hiko Seijuro
Hiten Mitsurugi-Ryu
Himura Kenshin

The Rurouni Kenshin Companion

Companion

Rival Character's Secrets

Name: **Udo Jin-e**
Occupation: **Retired assassin.**

Jin-e is a master swordsman who uses the Nikaido Heiho style. He worked as an assassin for both the Shinsengumi and the Ishin faction. In the story, he is introduced as a ruthless killer who targets former Ishin activists that are now prominent politicians and bureaucrats. Because he always hides his face behind a black, bamboo hat, he is also as known as 'Kurogasa' (black hat).

Jin-e is itching to fight Kenshin but is dissatisfied with him as an opponent because he follows the path of non-killing. Therefore Jin-e kidnaps Kaoru to provoke Kenshin to revert to his 'Hitokiri Battosai' persona. Disabled by Kenshin's Soryusen attack, Jin-e ultimately kills himself, leaving behind the ominous words: 'Once a killer, always a killer.'

鵜堂刃衛

41 Jin-e seems to enjoy killing, but is this really the case?

Unlike Kenshin, who killed out of his belief that it would help create a new era, Jin-e seems to truly enjoy the assassin's trade. When he first appeared in Kyoto during the Bakumatsu, he worked for the Shinsengumi. He killed countless Ishin activists, but because he habitually killed unnecessarily, the Shinsengumi tried to execute him. Jin-e fled, and some months later showed up on the opposite side of the conflict, working for the Ishin. So, for him killing is probably not exactly a tedious chore -he really does like it. Even so, there is some method to his madness. For instance, his 10-year, nationwide killing spree was in fact ordered by the Meiji government's military executives. In the end, Jin-e takes one last job -the assassination of himself on government orders to 'protect state secrets'. If he was captured alive, facts the government would prefer remain hidden might come to light, and an assassin must never reveal the identity of the person who requested the assassination. For these reasons, Jin-e complies with his employer's orders

See Glossary
Himura Kenshin
Shinsengumi
Meiji Ishin

See questions
1

and chooses death. In this sense, he was an assassin par excellence.

42 What is the Nikaido Heiho style?

Nikaido Heiho is a unique fighting style in which the opponent is attacked in three stages, represented by the kanji for the numbers 1 (一), 8 (八) and 10 (十). The sword strokes of this technique look like these characters, and when performed together form the 'Hei' (平) part of 'Heiho' (stack the kanji for 1 on top of 10, then flip the 8 on its head and insert it between them). However, this style's strange and terrifying Shin no Ippo techniques are more widely known than its fencing moves. Shin no Ippo, which at first glance looks like black magic, can paralyze opponents. It actually uses hypnosis and suggestion, and uses the force of the wielder's will, transmitted through the eyes, to paralyze opponents. This technique is also called Isukumi, and a master like Jin-e can use it to paralyze or inhibit the lungs. Furthermore, he can use the technique on himself to bring out all of his potential. This is called Hyoki no Jutsu. Because Jin-e truly believes he is stronger, he actually becomes stronger.

See Glossary
Nikaido Heiho
Shin no Ippo
Hyoki no Jutsu

Name: **Onmitsu Oniwabanshu**
Occupation: **Takeda Kanryu's bodyguards.**

Originally in charge of policing Edo Castle, they joined with Kanryu after the destruction of the castle during the Ishin. They are on a quest to attain the title of 'strongest'. There are five members: the leader, Shinomori Aoshi, Beshimi, Hannya, Hyottoko, and Shikijo. All four subordinates are killed protecting Aoshi from Kanryu's Gatling gun.

隠密御庭播衆

43   *What are the Oniwabanshu?*

The historical Oniwabanshu were originally spies and a type of ninja (or shinobi). They acted as guards and were hidden throughout the castles and mansions of the Shogun and Daimyo. In Rurouni Kenshin, the group headed by Aoshi was in charge of protecting Edo Castle, where the Shogun resided, and was therefore composed of the most experienced warriors. Originally, the group had 10 members, half of which were given government jobs by the Meiji administration after the Ishin. The remaining 4, along with their proud leader, had no particular skills other than fighting, and thus came to be employed as bodyguards by Kanryu.

See Glossary
Takeda Kanryu

44 How did the Oniwabanshu wind up in the Rurouni Kenshin universe?

There is actually an interesting story behind the appearance of the Oniwabanshu in Rurouni Kenshin. Nobuhiro Watsuki had originally written the story so that Kenshin fights Kanryu's private army of lackeys. However, the editor of the magazine carrying Rurouni Kenshin complained that he was sick of seeing Kenshin beat up on glorified street punks. So, it came to pass that Watsuki had to hastily assemble a group of elite fighters to defend Kanryu. Watsuki drew his inspiration from history, loosely basing the group on the historical Oniwabanshu.

See Glossary
Takeda Kanryu

Beshimi is certainly one of the lower ranked Oniwabanshu both in terms of status and raw power. His Rasenbyo dart techniques are not exactly threatening, inflicting at best a bit of pain (unless he uses poison). So it's a bit odd that a lowly spy like Beshimi was recruited for the elite Edo Castle Oniwabanshu. It seems he was hand-picked by Aoshi. Aoshi always recruited people he knew he could trust, and his instincts are proven to be correct when Beshimi gives up his life to protect him at the end of the Kanryu story. It is also possible that seeing Beshimi, a man with no real advantages, working hard to master his profession, Aoshi was impressed and wanted to give him a shot at a prestigious post. Aoshi is in fact a very caring character who looks after his subordinates (despite his vendetta against Kenshin, which turns him into a revenge-obsessed monster in the latter half of the story, leading him to kill even his old mentor Kashiwazaki Nenji). It is this concern for his underlings that leads him to take employment with the likes of Kanryu; he simply can not

See Glossary

Beshimi
Oniwabanshu
Rasenbyo
Shinomori Aoshi
Takeda Kanryu
Kashiwazaki Nenji

abandon his 4 unemployable subordinates for a cushy government job. Otherwise, a man like Aoshi would have done well under the new regime (in fact, he turns down several government job offers). The care and consideration he shows towards his underlings probably goes a long way towards explaining why he chose an underdog like Beshimi for the Edo Castle Oniwabanshu.

See questions
35

Hannya fled from his family when he was very young. He was from a poor village, and his family was about to kill him because they couldn't afford to raise him. It was at this point that Hannya met Aoshi, who raised him to become a top spy. Since disguise is of utmost important to spies, Hannya erases his own face by burning off his lips, lopping off his ears and nose, and breaking his cheekbones, in order to create a blank slate that can be disguised as any face with ease. These rather extreme actions reflect Hannya's respect for Aoshi, who raised him to be a master spy, and Hannya's desire to perform to perfection any spy work ordered by Aoshi.

Further, in order to perform his Shinwan no Jutsu technique, Hannya has tattooed both his arms with a horizontal stripe pattern, creating the illusion that they can stretch and lengthen. Hannya's exemplary dedication to his job has led him to alter his very body.

At one point it's mentioned that when Misao was still a child, Hannya doted on her more than any-

See Glossary

Hannya
Shinomori Aoshi
Shinwan no Jutsu
Makimachi Misao

one else. Despite his fearsome appearance, Hannya has a kind and loyal personality.

On another note, in Hannya's poignant childhood backstory, Watsuki again shows his talent for drawing on history to make his characters come to life. In the late Edo period, a series of famines struck Japan, and the practice of 'kuchiberashi', or 'reducing the number of mouths to feed' was common. In addition to killing or selling children into indentured servitude, the elderly were also sometimes taken into the mountains and left to die (a practice called 'ubasute').

47 Does Hyottoko's fire breathing technique have any basis in reality?

In Japanese Noh theater Hyottoko is a very old category of masks depicting a funny little man with a puckered mouth. The mask's name, Hyottoko, is a corruption of the word 'Hi-otoko' (fire man), in reference to the fact that the mask's expression looks like that of a man blowing on kindling to start a fire. Watsuki, however, took this word and interpreted it literally to mean a man who breathes fire, resulting in a character that looks something like a sumo wrestler. In fact he has to be huge to accommodate the oil bag he keeps in his belly and uses to perform the fire trick. His sumo wrestler appearance may also account for his empty-handed fighting style, which is called Toshukuken. While there may have been fire eaters in the early Meiji period who could produce a brief flame from oil held in the mouth (like Kiss's Gene Simmons), there were probably none capable of spewing out huge volumes of fire like Hyottoko.

S ee Glossary
Hyottoko
Toshukuken

48 What is the esoteric Oniwabanshu method Shikijo used to build up his muscles?

Shikijo's incredible brute strength allows him to hurl around big iron shot-puts with ease. His entire body is one, big mass of muscle. He actually obtained these muscles using a secret Oniwabanshu formula. The formula is never explained in detail in the manga, so we don't know if it's an ointment, some kind of pill, or just a protein/calcium-rich power-shake. Perhaps he's similar to Sanosuke in this respect (elsewhere we speculated that Sanosuke gets his super-resilient body from calcium in the fish bones he chews after every meal).

See Glossary
Oniwabanshu
Shikijo
Sagara Sanosuke

49 Why is Shinomori Aoshi so hung up on the title of 'strongest'?

Aoshi becomes the leader of the Oniwabanshu at the tender age of 15. It was a great honor for someone so young. However, during the time Aoshi was policing Edo Castle, the Ishin started. Yoshinobu, the final Tokugawa Shogun, perhaps realizing he was out-matched, turned his back on the many soldiers risking their lives for him and fled to Kaneiji Temple in Ueno. Without the Shogun around, there was no point in having a battle for Edo Castle, and it was taken bloodlessly. In terms of the Rurouni Kenshin story, this means that the Oniwabanshu weathered the Bakumatsu without ever having a chance to display their skills in battle.

Of course, without a Bakufu, the Oniwabanshu were out of a job too. For Aoshi to receive such a prestigious position, only to have his career end before he could demonstrate his skills, must have been an enormous blow to his ego. Kenshin, for example, had proved his mettle and left behind the legend of the Hitokiri Battosai. By comparison, the Oniwabanshu had done nothing of note and had left behind nothing worthy of posterity.

Therefore, Aoshi was intent on earning the title of

S ee Glossary
Shinomori Aoshi
Oniwabanshu

'strongest' for the Oniwabanshu to ensure their place in history. He believes that by defeating the Hitokiri Battosai, the greatest swordsman to ever live, they will earn this title.

When Beshimi, Hyottoko, Shikijo and Hannya sacrifice themselves to protect Aoshi, this preoccupation becomes even greater. He feels the only thing he can do to honor them is to obtain the posthumous title of 'strongest men' for them. He does not merely want glory for himself, but for his dead comrades, which is why he is obsessed with defeating Kenshin to the point of madness.

See Glossary
Beshimi
Hyottoko
Shikijo
Hannya

See questions
1 **2**

50 Is it true that Aoshi is based on a real person?

According to Watsuki, Shinomori Aoshi is based on Toshizo Hijikata (1835-1869), cofounder and second in command of the Shinsengumi. Although Hijikata was legendary for fighting right up until his death in battle, it is said he was actually a weak man who suppressed his true feelings and put on a demonic persona for the sake of his group. Watsuki seems to have used only the more heroic aspects of Hijikata's character in his portrayal of Aoshi. Hijikata was killed leading the remnants of the Shinsengumi in a final attack against the Ishin forces.

See Glossary
Shinomori Aoshi
Hijikata Toshizo

See questions
33

The Kodachi is a sword with a blade shorter than that of a normal katana. While less lethal than a normal sword, its speed makes it excellent for defense. Aoshi usually uses this sword in place of a shield while attacking with kempo techniques, but the Kodachi comes into play during his special moves, such as the Kaiten Kenbu. In this attack, Aoshi combines kempo and his Kodachi to create an original technique. He moves fluidly, circling to keep his opponent disoriented, allowing him to strike when least expected. Normal kempo attacks are performed from set stances, creating a clear division between 'static' and 'dynamic' moves. In contrast, the Kaiten Kenbu has no 'static' component, making it difficult for even a master swordsman like Kenshin to defend against.

Ultimately, Aoshi is unable to defeat Kenshin, even with the Kaiten Kenbu, so he cloisters himself in the forest to hone his skills. When he emerges, he carries two Kodachi and has a bag of new tricks to use against Kenshin. The extra sword

See Glossary

Shinomori Aoshi
Kodachi
Kaiten Kenbu

allows him to perform a two-sword version of the Kaiten Kenbu in addition, to attacking with swords crossed (Onmyo Kosa), or throwing them consecutively so that the first sword blocks the opponent's view of the second sword (Onmyo Hasshi).

Name: **Isurugi Raijuta**
Occupation: **Master Swordsman.**

石動雷十太

Founder of the Shinkoryu movement, which rejected the sport of fencing with bamboo swords that began to gain popularity during the early Meiji period, and sought to revive the traditional sword arts. As a former samurai, he uses his knowledge of swords to become a sword dealer under the patronage of Tsukuyama, a merchant who sells to foreign buyers.

52 What's Raijuta's motivation for destroying dojos?

Under the Meiji government, the occupation of 'warrior' ceased to exist, and the carrying of swords by the common people (ex-samurais included) was made illegal. The focus of the sword arts shifted from combat to sport, using bamboo swords (shinai). For instance, at Kaoru's Kamiya dojo, Yahiko always uses a shinai, and when Kaoru teaches at other dojos, she and her pupils are shown with shinai too. Raijuta, as the founder of the Shinkoryu movement, which is obsessed with ancient sword techniques and uses real swords, cannot bear to see fencing turned into a sport. In an effort to stop the spread of recreational fencing, he harasses the dojos where it's taught.

See Glossary
Ishurugi Raijuta
Kamiya Kaoru
Myojin Yahiko

53 What does Raijuta's Shinkoryu movement do?

Raijuta discovers an ancient book describing an old style of fencing called 'Koryu'. He spends 10 years learning its secret techniques. He creates the Shinkoryu movement specifically to spread the secrets of this ancient style in the modern age. These secrets consist of the 'Izuna' techniques, which involve swinging the sword very fast and using the resulting air pressure to perform attacks such as the Matoi Izuna and Tobi Izuna. In the Matoi Izuna, a vacuum trails behind the tip of the sword, increasingly enhancing the damage it does, so that a very prease cut can be produced even with a bamboo sword. The Tobi Izuna can send pressure waves flying towards the opponent. Although the Izuna techniques themselves are quite advanced, because Raijuta mastered them intellectually through reading, he is no match for Kenshin, who has real combat experience.

See Glossary
Ishurugi Raijuta
Shinkoryu
Matoi Izuna

Name: **Makoto Shishio**
Occupation: **Former assassin**

志々雄真実

An Ishin supporter from the Choshu region. He came out of the shadows to take over Kenshin's role in fighting the Shinsengumi and other Bakufu forces, succeeding Kenshin as 'Hitokiri Battosai'. Rumored to have been killed in the Boshin wars 10 years prior to the story arc. In fact, it was the government that tried to kill him because he knew too many secrets. However, he survived, although badly burned in the process, and now heads a vast coalition of blood-thirsty hawks and peace-hating arms dealers. Setting up a base in the Kyoto underworld, he capitalizes on secrets learned during his former job as assassin and plots a war of vengeance that will split Japan in two. His underlings are a group of mainly ruthless and ambitious warriors called the Juppon Gatana.

Kenshin spent the latter half of his employment with the Ishin faction working as a guerilla, leaving the position of 'Hitokiri' vacant. Shishio was selected to fill that role, and he proceeds to kill substantially more people than even Kenshin.

With the success of the Ishin, a new government was created and most of the important posts filled by Ishin supporters. Among these were many who had requested assassinations from Shishio. Fearing Shishio will use this information against them, they have him killed and then cremate his ostensibly lifeless body. However, Shishio miraculously survives, although hideously burned.

Shishio thus becomes consumed by revenge, but his wrath extends beyond just those who tried to kill him. Behind his motivation for initiating another revolution is a deep mistrust of the people at the top of the new government, who give no thought to killing others to protect themselves.

Like Kenshin, Shishio was a patriot of the Ishin who fought under the belief that the next era

⑤ee Glossary
Shishio Makoto
Himura Kenshin

See questions
2

would be a better era. His motivation for affecting a regime change is not simply revenge; he wants to create an 'ideal society'. Unfortunately, in Shishio's ideal society, the only guiding principle is survival of the strongest.

55 | Why does Shishio take over Shingetsu Village?

Shingetsu is a tiny village of less than 20 people located a short distance from Numazu in Tokaido. Shishio and his gang attack the village, kill its police, and take it over. The government abandons the village, and has it erased from all official maps. It is primarily administered by Senkaku, one of Shishio's lackeys, but Shishio returns once in awhile.

So why does Shishio capture the place then barely spend any time there? The town is situated exactly halfway between Kyoto and Tokyo, the two centers of Meiji government. As a military base, it could be used to attack both Tokyo and Kyoto. However, it seems that Shishio's real motive for capturing the village is its volcanic hot springs, which he returns to use every six months or so. Shishio's burns cover his entire body, and even the doctors aren't sure what's keeping him alive. It could be that the natural hot springs are an important source of relief for his ravaged body. The circumstances make it difficult for Shishio to visit hot springs or spas in public, particularly since bathing in hot springs entails being naked and defenseless. To secure a place where he can bathe in peace, he takes over an entire village.

See Glossary
Shishio Makoto
ShingetuVillege
Senkaku

56 | What is the Ikedaya Incident that inspired Shishio's plan to burn down Kyoto?

I n attempting to bring about revolution in Japan, Shishio gets the idea of burning Kyoto from the Ikedaya Incident. This was a real incident that occurred in June 1864 at an inn called the Ikedaya. A group of extreme Ishin activist planned to set fire to Kyoto, then use the ensuing confusion as a diversion while they killed a number of pro-Bakufu officials and court nobles, then kidnapped the Emperor and took him to Choshu. While they were laying this plan, they were attacked by the Shinsengumi, which saved Kyoto from being burned. By protecting Kyoto, the Shinsengumi publicly demonstrated their unique power to society at large while simultaneously making the Ishin group look like a gang of terrorists. While this plan to burn Kyoto failed, Shishio was determined to make it succeed the second time around.

However, the plan was actually a smokescreen which Shishio intentionally leaked to the police so that a large number of officers would be diverted to Kyoto. Shishio then planned to attack Tokyo, which would be left relatively undefended, with

See Glossary
Shinsengumi
Rengoku

See questions
33

the Rengoku, his battleship. Although Shishio thought his plan subtle, Kenshin's keen insight sees through it, and Shishio's machinations are foiled.

57 Why is Shishio's sword flammable?

Shishio's blade, the Mugenshin, is the work of the smith who created Kenshin's Sakabato, Arai Shakku, during his 'killer sword' period. A normal sword will dull the more it's used, causing it to become less effective and requiring sharpening. On the other hand, the Mugenshin has a finely serrated edge. The serrations are razor sharp, so that its ability to cut does not dull, even after being used on many people.

These fine serrations also accumulate the body fat of the Mugenshin's victims. By directing a flame or spark at this collected fat, Shishio can ignite it. Using his flaming sword, Shishio develops the Homura Dama technique, which both cuts and burns his opponent.

See Glossary
Shishio Makoto
Mugenshin
Sakabato
Arai Shakku

See questions
8 **9**

58 | Why does Shishio burst into flames towards the end of his fight?

As a result of his horrific burns, Shishio has lost his sweat glands and is no longer capable of sweating. Having lost his means of regulating body temperature, his temperature will rise if he engages in any hard exercise. If he performs a strenuous exercise (such as fighting) for more than 15 minutes, he could overheat and die. His final battle with Kenshin continues for more than 15 minutes, and the fact that he has killed Komagata Yumi, a person who has given him love despite his maimed appearance, has probably worsened his temperature control problem even further. As a result his temperature rises to the point where he spontaneously combusts and dies. Although he survived being burned alive once, this time his luck runs out.

S ee Glossary

Shishio Makoto
Himura Kenshin
Komagata Yumi

Name: **Juppon Gatana**

Shishio's 10 underlings who are participating in his revolution and working with him. The members are Seta Sojiro, Yukyuzan Anji, Sadojima Houji, Sawagejo Cho, Iwanbo, Hariwa Hennya, Uonuma Usui, Saizuchi, Fuji and Honjo Kamatari.

十本刀

59 What is Seta Sojiro's Shukuchi technique?

Seta Sojiro is said to be the power behind the Juppon Gatana. His secret is speed. He uses the natural strength of his legs to suddenly accelerate from low speed to his top speed, instantly closing on his opponent. He moves so quickly, that it seems as if the distance between him and his opponent has physically shrunk (hence the name, which literally means 'shrinking ground').

Kenshin's Hiten Mitsurugi-Ryu is also known for its great speed, but even so Kenshin is tossed around by Sojiro.

His speed is so great, it evades even the Kuzuryusen. Further, because Sojiro never portrays any emotion other than happiness, it is impossible to guess what he is about to do by reading his facial expressions.

Sojiro uses this speed to carry out the assassination of Okubo Toshimichi. The murder of Okubo was an historical event, perpetrated by a samurai descendent from Ishikawa prefecture named Shimada Ichiro. In Rurouni Kenshin however, Sojiro uses his amazing speed to jump onto Okubo's carriage and murder him before Shimada.

See Glossary
Seta Sojiro
Shukuchi
Juppon Gatana
Hiten Mitsurugi-Ryu
Kuzuryusen
Okubo Toshimichi

See questions
10

60 Why doesn't Sojiro express any feeling other than happiness?

Sojiro was orphaned as a child, and raised by a very abusive foster family. It's said that people who have suffered extreme abuse as children lose all emotional expression, which seems to be the case for Sojiro. He found that if he kept smiling, the adults didn't bully him as much, and so he learned to constantly wear a blissful expression.

Some years ago, Sojiro helped Shishio escape when he was being pursued by Meiji government forces. In return, Shishio gave him a Wakizashi short sword with which Sojiro killed his foster family. Since then Sojiro has cooperated with Shishio and has adopted Shishio's survival of the fittest philosophy. However, Kenshin's radically different point of view disturbs him, and this along with Kenshin's unanticipated strength irritate Sojiro, so that he gradually starts to express other emotions. This allows Kenshin to read his movements and defeat him.

See Glossary
Seta Sojiro
Shishio Makoto
Wakizashi
Himura Kenshin

Anji is originally a compassionate Buddhist priest, dedicated to alleviating the suffering of the common people. He also takes care of Tsubaki, the daughter of the village headman who was killed in the Boshin wars. The new village headman holds the former headman in contempt, because his support for the Bakufu caused the village to lose favor with the new Meiji government. By extension the new headman also hates Tsubaki and Anji. However, the village temple is still under government protection, so he pretty much leaves them alone.

It is important to understand that historically, during the Edo period, Buddhism was the official religion of the Tokugawa Bakufu. Furthermore, Buddhism had become intertwined with Japan's indigenous Shinto religion, and Shinto shrines could often be found inside Buddhist temples. However, with the inauguration of the Meiji administration, the Emperor, who is associated with Shinto, became the new center of government. To increase the authority of the Emperor, the

See Glossary
Yukyuzan Anji

Shinbutsu-Bunri (separation of Shinto and Buddhism) laws were passed. These laws were ostensibly designed to simply separate Shinto shrines from Buddhist temples, but also had the ulterior motive of promoting the authority of the Shinto gods (and thus the new government) while denigrating the position of the Buddhist temples (a symbol of the old Bakufu). A consequence of this was a radical movement to expel Buddhism from Japan altogether. This movement was called the Haibutsu Kishaku (destroy the Buddha, destroy Shakyamuni) movement. It resulted in the fairly violent destruction of many Buddhist temples and ancient artifacts by gangs of Shinto zealots.

In the story of Rurouni Kenshin, this Haibutsu Kishaku movement spreads to Anji's village and leads to the destruction of his temple, during which Tsubaki is killed. This experience transforms the kindly Anji into a demonic killer.

62 Who is this Fudo Myo-o that Anji tries to emulate?

Fudo Myo-o is a fearsome and powerful Buddhist deity whose job is to exterminate demons and defend Buddhists. He also rains down heavenly wrath on sinners. When Anji's temple is burned down, resulting in the death of his ward Tsubaki, he ignores the Buddhist admonition to refrain from killing 'even a single insect' and slaughters the responsible villagers. He blames the government's 'Shinbutsu Bunri'(separation of Shinto and Buddhism) policy for the incident, and joins Shishio's plot to overthrow the Meiji administration. At the same time, as a priest he has vowed to work for the salvation of all people, but he concludes that some people just aren't worth saving. He identifies with Fudo Myo-o, particularly with this deity's role in dishing out divine retribution. So that he too can make the sinners repent, Anji trains for 10 years, and as a result masters the Futae no Kiwami.

See Glossary
Yukyuzan Anji
Futae no Kiwami

See questions
19 63

63 Why on earth would Anji teach the Futae no Kiwami to Sanosuke, a man he's just met?

Anji hates the Meiji government so much that he's willing to go along with Shishio's schemes. When he meets Sanosuke in the forest, he asks his opinion of the government. Sanosuke, whose former mentor was treacherously executed by the government responds: 'I hate them.' It is certain that Anji had no quarrel with this opinion. He might have even thought of Sanosuke as a potential ally in overthrowing the government. So, Anji is easily convinced to teach Sanosuke the Futae no Kiwami, which he had spent the last 10 years mastering.

S ee Glossary

Yukyuzan Anji
Sagara Sanosuke
Futae no Kiwami

See questions
19 62

64 Why is 'power over life and death' Anji's condition for helping Shishio?

Although Anji models himself after Fudo Myo-o and yearns to unleash heavenly wrath on the wicked, he is opposed to the needless killing of good Buddhists. Therefore, he makes 'power over life and death' his condition for helping Shishio. In other words, Anji is in charge of deciding who the Juppon Gatana can kill, and who they must let live. As the embodiment of Fudo Myo-o, Anji allows those he regards as beyond redemption to be killed, while extending the protection of the Buddha to those who he thinks can be saved. Anji invokes this condition when Usui tries to kill Misao. Usui complies, showing that the other members of the Juppon Gatana respect this arrangement.

 See Glossary

Yukyuzan Anji
Shishio Makoto
JUppon Gatana
Makimachi Misao

65 Why are there no scenes of Hoji fighting?

Hoji seems to be just a consultant for Shishio's revolution plans, and doesn't have any special fighting skills. His talent lies in strategy. Upon learning that the failed attack on Kyoto was just a diversion to give the Rengoku a chance to attack Tokyo, the Juppon Gatana (correctly) express concern that 7 of their members had been used as sacrificial pawns. To deflect criticism away fro Shishio, Hoji claims responsibility for the plan, and rips out 7 of his own fingernails as penance. This satisfies the Juppon Gatana, and their group unity is restored. It's quick thinking like this that makes Hoji indispensable to Shishio, who understands well that people with management abilities are crucial to his plan. This is why Hoji is a valuable member, and can contribute without ever going into combat.

See Glossary
Sadojima Hoji
Juppon Gatana
Shishio Makoto

Cho, 'The Sword Hunter', is an avid collector of unusual swords. He also likes to try out his toys on real people. This hobby, rather than ideology, is his main reason for participating in Shishio's revolution scheme. Therefore, after being captured by the police, unlike Hoji, who kills himself in prison without hesitation to protect the cause, Cho found it easy to go along with Saito's orders. However, Cho is not simply a selfish weapons collector; he can be quite sensitive at times. When Kamatari loses her (his) will to live, it is Cho that talks her out of suicide. It is also likely that Cho was to some extent attracted to Shishio's cause by the charisma of Shishio himself. Saito Hajime is also a charismatic leader, so maybe this is why Cho is so easily talked into following his orders.

See Glossary
Sawagejo Cho
Saito Hajime
Shishio Makoto

67 Hennya is beaten by Yahiko. Does that make him a wimp?

Hennya wears a strange bat suit, which allows him to hover in the sky, from where he drops bombs on his enemies. This makes him a tough opponent, since he stays safely out of range and can attack with impunity. However, to allow him to float higher and longer, he has to starve himself to keep his weight down. While this gives him an advantage in the air, it means he has little resilience against damage. This is not really a weakness, as long as he can stay airborne. Nonetheless, Yahiko's quick wits are allow him to find a way to attack him (Yahiko figures out that he can use a broken door to 'surf' Hennya's bomb blasts, giving him the high ground). So, it's probably not fair to Yahiko to categorize Hennya as a wimp. Rather, Yahiko's brains, rather than Hennya's weakness, account for his defeat.

See Glossary
Hiei
Jaganshi
Dark Tournament
Jaou Ensatsu Ken
Zeru

68 Did Usui always have such supernaturally good hearing?

I n a past fight with Shishio, Usui lost his eyes, but his hearing is so good that he is able to perfectly ascertain his surroundings anyway. What's more, he can hear his opponent's individual heartbeats, allowing him to make deductions about his/her psychological state. His excellent hearing is actually not an acquired ability, but was present even before he lost his eyes. He simply did not notice it. After losing his eyes, he had to rely on his ears more, which is when he first noticed how unusually well he could hear. He then trained himself to determine people's psychological state from listening to their bodies.

See Glossary
Uonuma Usui
Shishio Makoto

69 | What is Usui's condition for helping Shishio?

Usui has agreed to help Shishio under the condition that he can attack Shishio at any time to exact revenge for the loss of his eyes. Since Shishio is on the run from the government and has to hide all the time, Usui probably decided it was more efficient to stick with Shishio than it would be to try to keep track of him. Usui is pretty open about telling the other members of the Juppon Gatana that his motive is revenge against Shishio. In fact, Usui has no intention of following through with this. He knows he has no chance of defeating Shishio. However, his pride won't let him admit this, so he continues to claim he plans on some day killing Shishio. Usui is shocked to find that Saito Hajime is able to deduce all this from very little information. It damages Usui's pride even more to learn that there is someone who is even better at reading minds than him. In the end, Usui's high pride is his downfall.

See Glossary

Unomura Usui
Shishio Makoto
Juppon Gatana
Saito Hajime

Fuji's freakish size made him an outcast, and even led to an attempt on his life by the people of his region. An old man named Saizuchi saved him. From that point on, Fuji followed every order Saizuchi gave, leading to his participation in Shishio's revolutionary plot. Unfortunately, Saizuchi didn't save Fuji out of the goodness of his heart; he hoped to use the giant for his own profit, a fact of which Fuji is also aware. Even so, Fuji has never been shown any compassion, so being turned into a war machine doesn't really disagree with him. Fuji doesn't rebel against Saizuchi until the battle with Hiko Seijuro. Seijuro is the first person to face Fuji as a fellow human, causing the giant to break down weeping with gratitude. On the other hand, the Spirit World probably judged that not having a physical body would prove a hindrance to investigating demons in the human world. Therefore, when she becomes a detective's assistant, she comes to the human world in a human body. Thus, even people like Keiko, who don't have a sixth sense per se, can see her.

See Glossary
Saizuchi
Fuji
Hiko Seijuro

Kamatari looks like a hot babe, but is actually a guy in drag. In other words he is gay. In Japanese, gay men, transvestites, or even guys who are just kind of effeminate, are referred to as 'Okama', which is a homonym (uh, no pun intended) in Japanese for scythe (kama). Even the character's name, Kamatari, contains the component 'kama', which again ties into the whole Okama/kama pun, so we can safely say that this choice of weapon can be explained by Watsuki's rakish sense of humor. Kamatari's Okama (big scythe) is fairly heavy, combining a massive blade with a chain and counterweight. This huge weapon combined with Kamatari's girlish appearance probably lulls enemies into a false sense of security -how could such a cute girl possibly wield such a heavy weapon effectively? However, since Kamatari is really a strapping, burly guy, s/he has no problem twirling the massive blade like a cheer baton of death. In other words, by misdirecting opponents with his appearance, Kamatari gains a psychological edge. You'd think that the inhabi-

See Glossary
Honjo Kamatari

70 Why are Saizuchi and Fuji working together?

⑤ee Glossary
Honjo Kamatari

124

tants of the anime universe would have learned by now to never trust cute chicks with huge weapons.

Name: **Yukishiro Enishi**
Occupation: **Arms dealer**

Enishi is a man who lives only to avenge the death of his sister, Tomoe, who was killed by Kenshin. Under the slogan of 'Jinchu', Enishi gathers a group of like-minded people who have a score to settle with Kenshin, vowing to punish Kenshin in place of God. The other people participating in this Jinchu campaign are Gein, Kujiranami Hyogo, Inui Banjin, Otowa Hyoko, and Yatsume Mumyoi. Helping to manage the team is U Heiren, Enishi's right-hand man in the arms dealership.

雪代縁

72 How did Kenshin become romantically involved with Tomoe?

While working as an assassin, Kenshin is ordered to kill Shigekura Jubei, an official working in Kyoto. He kills Shigekura, along with his bodyguard, Kiyosato Akira. Kiyosato was the fiancé of Tomoe. Ironically, Kiyosato had put off their marriage to go to Kyoto and work as Shigekura's guard. He wanted the prestige the work offered, feeling it was unfair that Tomoe, a woman of such high standing, should be married to someone as lowly as himself. Vowing to take revenge on Kenshin for killing her fiancé, Tomoe becomes a spy in order to get close to him. However, as part of her spy work, she ends up living with Kenshin, and finds herself falling in love with him. Kenshin falls in love with her too, and that is how they end up married.

See Glossary
Shigeura JUbei
Kiyosato Akira

See questions
13

73 What is the Yaminobu?

The Yaminobu, which uses Tomoe as bait in their attempt to kill Kenshin, is an elite spy ring, probably equal in strength to Shinomori Aoshi's Oniwabanshu. They specialize in performing assassinations under the cover of darkness. The Yaminobu members who participate in the attack on Kenshin at Kekkai Forest are Sumita, Nakajo, as well as Yukishiro Enishi and Yatsume Mumyoi, who later lead the Jinchu campaign against Kenshin. Tatsumi is Inui Banjin's mentor, while Nakajo is a close friend of Otowa Hyoko. Inui and Otowa participate in the Jinchu campaign to avenge Tatsumi and Nakajo respectively.

See Glossary

Yaminobu
Yukishiro Tomoe
Shinomori Aoshi
Oniwabsnshu
Sumita
Nakajo
Yatsume Mumyoui
Ttshumi

74 Why does Kujiranami Hyogo have an Armstrong cannon for his right hand?

Hyogo's right hand was lopped off by Kenshin in a previous battle. Instead of an artificial limb, Hyogo replaces his arm with the powerful Armstrong cannon, which he uses to reduce Akabeko to rubble from a nearby mountain. This weapon is imported from abroad by Enishi. It is also considered one of the 3 Great Weapons of the Bakumatsu, and appears on Shishio's Rengoku. The recoil form this gun is so great, that it usually has to be mounted on a huge gun carriage. Even Hyogo's monstrous strength cannot absorb the shock, so he has to use massive trees to prop himself up when he fires it. Hyogo eventually trades the Armstrong cannon in for a custom grenade launcher, with which he terrorizes the town.

See Glossary
Kujiranamai Hyogo
Akabeko
Bakumatsu

75 Why is Kujiranami Hyogo still holding a grudge against Kenshin?

During the Ishin, Hyogo was a samurai who fought for the Bakufu, leading to the loss of his arm in a duel with Kenshin. During this duel, Hyogo already knew that the Bakufu's impending defeat was clear, and that the samurai were doomed. Therefore, he asked Kenshin to kill him, so that he could at least die like a samurai on the battlefield. However, Kenshin refused. This hurt Hyogo's pride, since it meant he would have to face the coming new age as a disabled, defeated warrior and live his life out in shame. Instead of facing up to the challenges ahead, he blames his shame and embarrassment on Kenshin for letting him live.

See Glossary
KujiranamiHyogo
Himura Kenshin

Muteki-ryu kempo, which is the forte of Inui and Yaminobu leader Tatsumi, is a martial art, similar to karate, that transforms the body into a lethal weapon. It draws together all the best aspects of martial arts from many eras and countries. Inui refines the Muteki-ryu style by incorporating the Tekko bracelets he receives from Enishi. The Tekko's angular surfaces can deflect the strongest swords and are thick enough to block even bullets. Inui uses them for attack and defense, and brags that they make him invincible. He can use them to perform unique moves, like the Ashura Guruma, in which he does a mid-air spin, striking with his entire body.

See Glossary
Muteki-Ryu
Inui Banshin
Yaminobu
Tattsumi
Raijin Gruruma
Ashurasai

Otowa keeps his weapons hidden on his body, so he can catch his opponents off guard. In all, he has 13 secret weapons hidden all over his body, including the Baika Chuzen, a weapon he keeps strapped to his arm that fires metal spears out of six barrels using a powerful spring. He can create a poisonous vapor with the Kasui Busuen, or impregnate his enemy with Bishamonpun, iron sand which helps guide his magnetic sword, the Bishamonken. Also, the gaudy hand-like thing attached to his coat is called the Rikudoko and it's actually a weapon. Though not exactly concealed, it's camouflaged making it harder to notice.

See Glossary

Otowa Hyoko
Baika Chuzen
Kasui Busuen
Bishamonpun
Bishamonken
Rikudoko

Yatsume Mumyoi was born into the Yatsume clan of gold miners who belong to the Kanahorishu, a group that excavates a gold vein that has funded war efforts throughout generations of leaders. There was fierce competition within the group to efficiently mine the limited gold supply, and each family had its own secret methods. In Yatsume no Jintaiseisei, gold bracelets are fit around the arms and legs of newborn children. As the child grows, the number of bracelets is increased, stretching their arms and legs to give them an advantage when mining gold in the narrow subterranean caves. This is a trade secret of the Yatsume clan, which has many rivals in the Kanahorishu. Consequently, the fact that their arms and legs are elongated means they must keep themselves hidden from sight. During the battle of Kekkai Forest, Kenshin sees Mumyoi with his arms and legs extended. As a result, Mumyoi wants to kill Kenshin to keep the Yatsume's clan secret safe, which is why he participates in the Jinchu campaign.

Even when the other Jinchu members meet in Yokohama, Mumyoi refuses to show himself in accordance with his clan's policy.

The Yatsume clan has mined gold for generations, but gold is a finite resource. The vein eventually starts to run out. In fact, there is none left by Mumyoi's generation. Looking around for a new career, Yatsume decides to put his stretched limbs to use as a spy. This work probably appealed to him, since spies mostly operate in the dark, reducing the danger of his family secret being revealed. This is how he comes to join the Yaminobu. His time with the Kanahorishu has provided him with a rich set of tools that make him a good spy. For instance, he can perform special attacks with his elongated limbs, dig and hide in holes, and is used to handling explosives.

Japan has a long tradition of mechanical dolls, which used springs to move. Some of the dolls, such as one that would pour your tea and bring it to you, were the precursor of the modern robot in terms of sophistication. Gein is descended from a long line of doll-makers who built such mechanical dolls. His use of the title 'artist' shows Gein's rather strong egoism, and he lives for the challenge of building ever more elaborate creations to show off to the world. He takes part in both Shishio's revolution scheme and Enishi's Jinchu campaign. His motive for helping them is simply that cutting-edge technology is always developed for the battlefield, and he wants to hone his technical skills by staying in close proximity to the action. Iwanbo of the Juppon Gatana is actually a mechanical doll controlled from the inside by Gein. He keeps upgrading Iwanbo, finally creating the Sango Iwanbo incorporating his ideals of 'functional beauty'. He then takes it into battle against Kenshin. The Sango Iwanbo has joints that rotate 180 degrees, and can

See Glossary
Gein

be released so that Kenshin is unable to cut through them. It is a remarkable device, but it turns out to be too elaborate, and Kenshin is able to defeat it by simply jamming its gears with a small stone.

G ein succeeds in fooling Kenshin and the others into believing that Kaoru is dead by creating a replica corpse using bodies stolen from a graveyard. To do this, he uses a secret technique originally developed to create doubles of the Shogun called 'Geho Hijutsu'. This concept seems to be inspired by the historical use of kagemusha, or 'shadow warriors' who looked like the warlords they protected, to confuse enemies during Japan's Sengoku era. A kagemusha was also used as a stand-in when a warlord died, to keep the enemy from knowing. In Rurouni Kenshin,'Geho Hijutsu', is a method for creating a mannequin of the warlord while he is still alive. Corpses of other people are used to create an exact copy of the warlord. Gein is especially skilled at this grisly technique, and uses it to create a stunningly convincing copy of Kaoru, which Gein declares to be his greatest creation ever. Wanting his masterpiece back, Gein tries to steal it from the grave where it's interred, only to be ambushed and killed by Aoshi.

See Glossary
Gein
Himura Kenshin
Kamiya Kaoru
Geho Hijutsu

See questions
80

Other works of Rurouni Kenshin

The original Rurouni Kenshin manga spawned an animated series, broadcast by Fuji Television, movie, and original videos.

Movie
Rurouni Kenshin: Ishin Shishi no Requiem (1997)
The movie featured an original story that appeared neither in the manga nor the anime series. Visiting Yokohama, Kenshin meets Takimi Shigure, a man from the former Aizu province. Takimi wants to lead a revolt against the government, leading to an inevitable showdown with Kenshin. Running time: 98 min.

Original Video
Rurouni Kenshin:Tsuiokuhen (Feb.-Sep. 1999, 4 volumes)
These four stories fill in details of the backstory to the original Rurouni Kenshin manga. The series tells the story of how Kenshin got his cross-shaped scar and climbed to No. 7 on the US Billboard video sales charts (under the US title of Samurai X). Unlike the popular manga and anime series, it was drawn in a serious style that vividly depicted the blood and chaos of the Bakumatsu era. The series was well received both in Japan and abroad, and helped establish Rurouni Kenshin's popularity

Rurouni Kenshin: Seis_hen (Dec. 2001 - Mar. 2002, 2 volumes)
This work takes place 10 years after the original series, giving a digest of intervening time. It is billed as a sequel to Recollection, taking up the theme of Kenshin's "atonement" for his past sins. It is the final chapter of the saga.

82 Can Gein fight without using Iwanbo?

Although a doll-maker with no combat skills, his years of manipulating his creations have made Gein very dexterous. This dexterity allows him to perform a technique called Geho Kuriito no Jutsu, in which he uses fine, steel wires to attack his opponent. Particularly deadly is his Kika Hachiho Inojin technique, in which he ensnares his opponent with the oil impregnated by steel wires, then ignites the wire, burning his victim to death.

🄢 ee Glossary
Gein
Geho Kurito no Jutst

83 Who is U Heiren?

U Heiren is second in command of Yukishiro Enishi's secret arms import company, and has probably contributed to expanding the company considerably. Since Enishi can't really manage the company while pursuing his Jinchu campaign, it stands to reason that U Heiren is in charge of running it. However, U Heiren is quite critical of Enishi's Jinchu activities, complaining that they'll draw even more attention from the police than they've been getting already. U Heiren see's himself simply as Enishi's business partner, and wants nothing to do with the Jinchu campaign.

84 Who are the Sushin?

U Heiren is not a fighter, so he has a group of four bodyguards, the Sushin, that accompany him constantly. Their names come from the mythical guardians for the 4 directions: Suzaku, the bird, guards the South, the white tiger Byakko guards the West, the dragon Seiryu guards the East, and Genbu the turtle guards the North. While the four normally follow U Heiren closely, at his command they will leap into battle. All four can jump amazingly high, are armed with a weapon, and can assess their opponent's abilities and determine the optimal attack at a glance. Their weapons are: the Fen Gimu (Suzaku), Daito (Seiryu), Chemu Kun (Byakko) and Sei Kuan (Genbu). They also have very keen eyes for detail. When Seiryu faces Aoshi, he's able to tell Aoshi is carrying an extra concealed Kodachi, rather than one long sword, just by looking at the hilt and scabbard. Among the Sushin, Seiryu actually has the keenest ability to foresee his opponents' moves. For example, he recognizes the weakness of Saito Hajime's Gatotsu. Byakku specializes in

See Glossary
U heiren
Sushin
Suzaku
Seiryu
Byakko
Gnbu

See questions
83

Paafu Chie Mukun, which uses the most appropriate form for different target areas, making it effective against even big game like tigers. It has many variations, including the Koso, Sassho, Takushi, Gotogoku, etc. Byakko's Chemu Kun are his most powerful weapon. Suzaku is an expert at copying the moves of his opponent and making them his own. Genbu has the most conservative fighting style of the group. His weapon looks like a simple staff, but can actually turn into nunchaku.

After Tomoe dies, Enishi can no longer stand being in Japan and leaves for Shanghai, China. However, he has no friends or family there, and the city is crawling with mafia. Within a few weeks, he is on the verge of starving, but is rescued by a Japanese couple. They take pity on Enishi not only because he's so young, but also because he's a fellow Japanese expatriate, and take him back to their house where they care for him. Enishi is saved from certain death, but instead of thanking the couple, he kills them and steals their money. In the house of the unfortunate couple, Enishi finds a book on fencing, which he studies and masters. After joining the Shanghai mafia, he eventually starts his own arms dealership.

See Glossary
Yukishio Tomoe
Yukishiro Enishi

86 | What is Watojutsu?

Between the 13th and 18th centuries, pirates transversed the inland sea around Japan. Eventually, they crossed over to the China coast. The Ming administration fought against these pirates, and through these battles Japanese style swords for close combat were introduced to China. Eventually, a warrior-monk of the Shaolin temple named Teiso Kahn began to research these pirates and their swords, and produced a book on short swords. Another Chinese military leader, Sekikeiko, quickly adopted the Japanese sword in his regiment. Eventually, the late Ming dynasty formally adopted the Japanese swords. In addition to importing the blades, unique continental versions were also produced. This Chinese adaptation of the Japanese sword was called the Wato (Wo Dao), and Watojutsu is the art of using it. This style fuses the speed and sharpness of Japanese blades with the grace and power of mainland martial arts and is distinguished by its dynamism. Enishi learns Watojutsu during his time in China.

See Glossary
Watojutsu
Teiso Kahn
Sekikeiko

87 What is Kyokei Myaku?

Enishi's hatred of Kenshin, which he cannot forget for even an instant, keeps him in a constant state of heightened tension. As a result, his nervous system never rests, and his nerves have thickened. This condition is called Kyokei Myaku, and when Enishi grows agitated, his nervous system kicks in with a vengeance. This gives Enishi better hearing, vision and reaction time than normal people, making his opponent's movements seem slow from his point of view. While Kenshin draws on his experience to read what his opponent is about to do, Enishi can actually watch his opponent to determine his next move, then react quickly due to his heightened reflexes. However, his nerves are a bit too sensitive, and high frequency sounds can disorient him, causing him to lose his balance.

See Glossary
Kyokei MYaku
Yukishiro Enishi
Himura kenshin

GLOSSARY
AND
KEYWORD
INDEX

GLOSSARY(CAST)

A

Akane
Used as collateral on a debt, like Kenshin she is sold to slavers at a young age. Killed by bandits.

Akamatsu Arundo
One of Shibumi's hand-raised assassins. Uses a sickle and weighted chain. Killed along with Shibumi by Saito Hajime.

Ameuri no Yoita (Candyman Yoita)
Delinquent buddy of Sanosuke. Dies from opium addiction a month before the opening of the story arc.

Arai Azura
Arai Seiku's wife. Iori's mother. Has a lovely forehead.

Arai Iori
Arai Seiku's infant son. Only speaks baby-talk. Taken hostage by Cho Comes to his senses. Later, he enters a private junior high, and leads the life of a normal student. His power is Gamemaster.

Arai Seiku
Arai Shakku's son. A swordsmith like his father, but only makes kitchen knives and pots due to his peace-loving personality. Lives with his wife and child.

Arai Shakku
Creator of the Sakabato. Deceased. Bakumatsu swordsmith who was ostracized by the sword-making community due to his obsession with creating 'lethal blades'. He created the Sakabato out of regret over making killing blades, giving it to Kenshin as a farewell gift.

B

Beshimi
Beshimi: Low ranking Oniwabanshu spy. Somewhat weak and timid, he specializes in the use of Rasenbyo throwing darts. Killed with the other Oniwabanshu trying to protect Aoshi from Kanryu's Gatling gun.

C

Chauchau Girls
3 Kyoto girls. Yahiko goes into culture

shock hearing their conversation (which sounds like 'Chau? Chau? Chau?') Reappear with the job of passing letters from Aoshi to Okina.

Cho Tsurahide
Former samurai from Ishikawa prefecture who assisted in Okubo's assassination.

Chuetsuryu Maekawa Dojo
Dojo where Kaoru used to give lessons. The instructor is Maekawa Miyauchi, an old friend of Kaoru's dad.

Cross-shaped scar
The scar on the left side of Himura Kenshin's face. It was given to him by Kiyosato Akira and Yukishiro Tomoe.

D

Dobuita Nagaya
Tenement where Tsukioka Tsunan lives. It's in the adjacent town.

E

F

Fuji
Does all the heavy lifting for the Hagun. Freakishly large. Hiko Seijuro is the first person to treat him as a fellow warrior, not a monster. Loses to Hiko Seijuro of his own volition. Becomes a colonist in Hokkaido.

Fujita Tokia
Fujita Goro's (Saito Hajime) wife. Formerly from Aizu. A very reliable woman.

G

Gasuke
A member of the Kant? Shueigumi yakuza. Nick-named 'Hitokiri Wasuke'. Kenshin easily defeats him.

Gein
Last in a long line of mechanical doll-makers. Joins with Shishio and Enishi, under the logic that cutting-edge technology is always developed for the battlefield. One of the central players in the Jinchu campaign, along with Enishi. Creates a phony Kaoru corpse. Killed by Aoshi.

Ginji

Delinquent buddy and gambling partner of Sanosuke. Seriously injured by Beshimi.

Goro
An orphan who lived at Jurakuji. The youngest, he's often bullied by Tasuke.

Gorotsuki Nagaya
The name of the tenement where Sanosuke lodges. Located on the out-skirts of town.

Great Kyoto Fire
Shishio's plot, modeled on the historical "Ikedaya Incident", to burn down Kyoto. In fact only a diversion from his real plan to attack Tokyo with the battle-ship Rengoku (Purgatory). The fire itself is controlled by the police, the Kyoto Oniwabanshu, and the townspeople.

H

Hachisuka
Leads the Hishimanji Gurentai thugs. Attacks the Kamiya Dojo, where Sato-kun and Hira-chan are hiding, with a wooden cannon.

Hakubaiko
The brand of hair oil Tomoe uses. It is sold in Nakamachi, of the Ikenobata area (now the Taito-ku ward of Tokyo).

Hannya
The Oniwabanshu's emissary. Uses kempo. Keeps his face hidden behind a mask. His signature move is the Shinwan no Jutsu, which employs an optical illusion. He has tattooed both his arms, creating the illusion that they are shorter than they actually are. This trick works well for hitting opponents like Kenshin who are good at dodging. His true face is hideous and featureless. Since disguise is of utmost important to spies, Hannya burns off his lips, cuts off his ears and nose, and breaks his cheekbones, in order to create a blank slate that can be disguised as any face. Hannya was from a poor village, and fled from his family, when they were about to kill him because they couldn't afford to raise him. It was at this point that Hannya met Aoshi, who raised him to become a top spy. Killed protecting Aoshi from Kanryu's Gatling gun. Doted on Misao before the Oniwabanshu began working for Kanryu.

Harada Sanosuke (1840-1868)
Shinsengumi Assistant Vice Commander.

Heishin Bussan

Trade company run by Enishi's crew as a front. The company warehouse is at the mouth of the Arakawa River.

Higashidani Kamishimoemon

Sanosuke's father. A simple radish farmer, he stands up to Fudosawa, who is trying to take over the town. His field is wiped out by Fudosawa's sabotage, so he just switches from growing radishes to mushrooms. Defeats 50 of Fudosawa's lackeys, but is losing the battle again the onset of middle-age.

Higashidani Naname

Sanosuke's mother. Loses her health and dies after giving birth to Ota, 2 years before the story arc.

Higashidani Uki

Sanosuke's younger sister. Overprotective of her little brother Ota, due to the trama of losing her brother's disappearance and her mother's death by illness.

Hiko Seijuro

Kenshin's master, and the 13th successor of the Hiten Mitsurugi-ryu's secret techniques. Self-confident for good reason, he is probably the strongest man in the Rurouni Kenshin universe. Wily,

blunt and misanthropic.

Hijikata Toshizo (1835-1869)

Shinsengumi Vice Commander.

Himura Kenji

Son of Himura Kenshin and Kaoru. Never really gets close to his father Kenshin.

Himura Kenshin

An Ishin patriot from Choshu, active during the Bakumatsu. He was known as the 'Hitokiri Battosai'. After the Ishin victory at Toba Fushimi, he disappears, renouncing killing to become a wanderer . He has a short, lean build and a cross-shaped scar on the left side of his face. He comes to stay at the Kamiya Dojo during the 'false Battosai incident'.

Hira-chan

Former student at the Kamiya Dojo. Picks a fight with the Hishimanji Gurentai while drunk, causing a lot of trouble for the dojo. Has an injured shoulder.

Hiruma Gohei

A thorough rogue of huge proportions who takes over the Kiheikan and rules it oppressively. Posing as the Battosai, he goes on a rampage in an attempt to defame the Kamiya Dojo, but is defeated by the real Battosai (Kenshin). After being arrested, he and his brother escape prison and hire Zanza (a.k.a. Sanosuke) in an attempt at revenge against Kenshin. After that, the two end up in Shinshu, where they mooch off Onitaoshi no Fudosawa.

Hiruma Kihei

Pretends to be a kindly old man. He feigns passing out so that Kaoru rescues him, and works as her servant, but it's all part of the 'false Battosai' ploy. He and his brother Gohei conspire to try to rob the Kamiya Dojo of its land, but Kenshin interrupts their plot and the two are arrested. After escaping prison, he and his brother hire Zanza (a.k.a. Sanosuke) to avenge Kenshin's meddling. After that, they flee the capital for Shinshu and freeload off of Onitaoshi no Fudosawa.

Hishimanji Gurentai

An organization of criminals even less restrained and more vicious than the Yakuza. They attack the Kamiya Dojo, in which Hira-chan and Sato-kun are hiding, with a crude cannon, but are repulsed.

Honjo Kamatari

A transvestite who wields a huge scythe. Yumi's rival maybe? Loses to Kaoru and Misao. Looses her will to live after Shishio's death, but Cho's lie cheers her up. Scheduled to pose as a female student and travel overseas as a government spy.

Hyottoko

Mid-ranked Oniwabanshu. A mountain of a man who carries a barrel strapped to his back. He can become a human flame-thrower with his Kaen Toiki Kaen Toiki attack by regurgitating oil from a bag he keeps in his stomach and igniting it with his flinty teeth. This is his only skill though, and he loses to Sanosuke. Killed protecting Aoshi from Kanryu's Gatling gun.

I

Iizuka

A Choshu patriot who worked with the Battosai, but was secretly part of the Yaminobu. Killed by Shishio Makoto.

Imposter Battosai incident

A ploy by the Hiruma brothers to make off with the Kamiya Dojo's land. The older brother, Kihei, sneaks into the dojo, while the younger brother Gohei pretends to be the Battosai in order to ruin the reputation of Kamiya-ryu.

They're on the brink of successfully stealing the land when the real Battosai (Kenshin) appears, and ruins their plans.

Inferno Room
Shishio's arena. Located in the belly of a sheer cliff, it gives opponents no place to run.

Inui Banjin
Just a war-monger. Joins the Jinchu to avenge his master. Defeated by Sanosuke.

Ishiji
A guard. Killed by the Hitokiri Battosai while guarding Shigekura Jubei.

Itomi Kio
Seiyo Kijutsudan chairman. Author of the short-story 'The Bucket'.

Isurugi Raijuta
Uses Izuna techniques. Founds a neo-classical fencing movement in reaction against modern, sport fencing that uses bamboo swords. Learns some ancient techniques from a secret manual, but his skill is all style, and he knows nothing of actual combat. Kenshin beats him with a left-handed Hiryusen, after which Raijuta never regains his self-confi-dence.

Iwanbo
Actually a mechanical doll created by Gein. Gein controls it from inside. Has to flee during the attack on Aoi-ya when all his supporters are wiped out.

J

Jinchu: Retribution by human hands
The opposite doctrine of Tenchu (divine retribution). The slogan adopted by Yukishiro Enishi and his six followers in their quest for revenge against Kenshin.

Jugo Room
Anji's room in Shishio's hideout. Decorated with a statue of Fudo Myo-o (a wrathful Buddhist deity).

Juppon Gatana
Literally, the "10 Swords". Shishio Makoto's private army. There are 10 members: Sojiro, the blind Usui, Anji, Hoji, Cho, Henya, Kamatari, Iwanbo, Saizuchi, and Fuji.

Jurakuji Temple
Anji's temple in Hokkaido. Though it had no parishioners, a number of

orphans lead a self-sufficient life there. During the persecution against Buddhism that occurred during the early Meiji period, the temple was burned down by a group lead by the village headman. The orphans died in the fire, but Anji survived although severely wounded.

Jushitai
A division of Takeda Kanryu's private army. Defeated before they have a chance to attack.

K

Kanahorishu
Group that excavates a gold vein that has funded war efforts throughout generations of leaders.

Kanto Shuei Gang
Yakuza gang lead by Tanishi that controls the lower part of Tokyo and recruits various pickpockets and rogues. Kenshin routs the entire gang when he comes to rescue Yahiko from their clutches.

Kanto Shuei Gang
Yakuza gang lead by Tanishi that controls the lower part of Tokyo and

recruits various pickpockets and rogues. Kenshin routs the entire gang when he comes to rescue Yahiko from their clutches.

Kamiya Kaoru
Koaru's father, Kamiya Koshijiro was called up to serve in the Seinan war, where he lost his life. Kaoru now keeps the Kamiya Dojo running by herself. During the 'imposter Battosai' incident, she loses her students, but later gets the dojo on back on its feet with Kenshin as a lodger and Yahiko as a student. She makes a living teaching at other dojos.

Kamiya Koshijiro
Kaoru's father. He creates the Kamiya Kasshin-ryu at the start of the Meiji era. However, as a member of the police battotai (sword unit), he had to serve in the Seinan war, where he lost his life.

Kariwa Henya
Can float in the air, dropping bombs on opponents from the sky. Defeated by Yahiko's Miyo Mimane Ryutsuisen. After being arrested, he cuts a deal and becomes a scout for the army, using his ability to survey the field from the sky.

Kashiwazaki Nenji
Aoi-ya owner and investigator for the Kyoto Oniwabanshu. Seems like a strange old man, but was actually very good with tonfa, and was next in line to head up the Oniwabanshu. Fights to stop the attack on Aoi-ya, but is seriously wounded.

Kasshin Shintoryu Kikuhara Dojo
A dojo in Echigo where Yahiko gives lessons. Kikuhara, a former student of Kaoru's father, runs the dojo.

Kasumi
Used as collateral on a debt, like Kenshin she is sold to slavers at a young age. Killed by bandits.

Katsura Kogoro
A real person. A significant Choshu leader. In Rurouni Kenshin, draws Kenshin onto the path of a Hitokiri.

Katagai
A Choshu activist. Close associate of Katsura. Stops Iizuka's betrayal with the Yaminobu, but is killed.

Kawaji Toshiyoshi (1834-1879)
A real person. Superintendent General of the Metropolitan Police. Formerly from Satsuma, he discovered Okubo's talents. Worked to modernize Japan's police after the Meiji era began. Shows up in Rurouni Kenshin as Okubo's escort.

Kekkai Forest
Magic forest with an odd magnetic field. This renders the Battosai's 'sixth sense' useless, which is why the Yaminobu chooses it as the location of the deciding battle.

Kenkakutai
A division of Takeda Kanryu's private army.

Kiheikan
A dojo in the outskirts of a town near the Kamiya dojo. A dojo in name only, it's more of a flophouse for gamblers and scoundrels. Hiruma Gohe temporarily takes over the Kiheikan, but Kenshin puts him in his place during the "imposter Battosai" incident.

Kikuhara Midori
Daughter of the owner of Kikuhara Dojo. Has a weak constitution and a spontaneous personality. Her real father holds an important post at the police headquarters.

Kitaki

Assistant inspector. Ends up at the Kikuhara Dojo while chasing Muto and company. Treats criminals like worms.

Kiyosato Akira

Second son of a lower-ranking vassal. Was the fiancé of Yukishiro Tomoe. Come to Tokyo to work as a guard in an attempt to make Tomoe happy. Killed by the Hitokiri Battosai while guarding Shigekura Jubei. Gave the Battosai part of the scar on his left cheek.

Kohagiya

One of the Choshu faction's hideouts. Formerly home to the Battosai.

Kondo Isami (1834-1868)

Shinsengumi director.

Komagata Yumi

Shishio's mistress. Former Yoshiwara courtesan. Disenchanted with the Meiji government's approach and at some point joins Shishio's movement. Falls on Shishio's sword in an attempt to give him an opening to defeat Kenshin.

Korosazu ("non-killing")

The philosophy Kenshin adopts after giving up the life of a killer and becoming a wanderer. He will fight when necessary, but has vowed to never kill again. The "reverse-blade" sword (sakabatto) he carries symbolizes this oath.

Koshotai

A division of Takeda Kanryu's private army. Responsible for Kanryu's personal safety.

Kujiranami Hyogo

Former Bakufu supporter. Loses his right arm to Kenshin in the battle of Toba-Fushimi. Joins the Jinchu campaign. Replaces his right arm with an Armstrong cannon, then with a grenade launcher. Loses his senses and goes on rampages. Finally brought down by Yahiko's bravery.

Kuma

An old soldier. Possibly of samurai lineage.

Kuro

Member of the Oniwabanshu. Works as a cook at Aoi-ya. Stocky character.

Kyoto Oniwabanshu

Group created to act as spies in Kyoto for the Oniwabanshu's information network. They work from Aoi-ya, a restaurant. Their weapons of choice are relatively lightweight.

Kyusoshu

Subordinates in Shishio's army who have unusually good night-vision and have been trained for night attacks. Their weapons of choice are metal claws. They try attacking Aoi-ya, but are repulsed.

L
M

Maekawa Miyauchi

Chuetsuryu Maekawa Dojo's master. Friend of Kaoru's father. Was once counted among the top 20 swordsmen of Edo, but is made fully aware of his age by being beaten by Raijuta and Banjin. Turns the dojo over to his successor and retires.

Makimachi Misao

Girl who Kenshin meets on his way to Kyoto. Daughter of the former Oniwabanshu head, she was taught kempo by Hannya. Adores Aoshi, but it's unknown if the feeling is mutual. Looks much younger than her actual age of 16. Straightforward personality.

Maria Luz Incident

An actual event, this was the first international trial involving Japan. A number of slaves escaped a Peruvian ship (the Maria Luz) docked in Yokohama. The Kanagawa prefectural authority and presiding judge over the case, Oe Taku, decided to release the slaves and repatriate them to their home countries. This incident lead to debate over the problem of women forced to work as geisha and prostitutes, and the establishment of the Geisha and Prostitute Freedom Act.

Meiji Ishin (1866-1869)

Japan's revolution, or "restoration" as it is often called. The ruling Tokugawa Bakufu, composed of the shogun and upper samurai, were challenged and ousted by a coalition that of the lower-ranked samurai, mainly for the Satsuma and Choshu provinces (the "Sat-cho alliance") and the Emperor was declared Japan's head of state. Events and characters of the Ishin, both true and fictional, form the back-story of the Rurouni Kenshin universe.

Mishima Eiji

A young man from Shingetsu Village. Wants to avenge the death of his parents on Senkaku, but is stopped by Kenshin. Currently in the care of Saito Hajime's wife.

Mishima Eiichiro
Spy and protégé of Saito. Sneaks into his hometown, Shingetsu Village, and flees with his younger brother Eiji. Severely wounded during the escape. Dies leaving Eiji in Kenshin's care.

Mt. Ueno
Position from which Kujiranami fires the Armstrong cannon, destroying Akabeko.

Myojin Yahiko
Born into a Tokyo family descended from samurai. His father was killed in the Ueno War and his mother died of illness. With no relatives left, Yahiko was forced to work as a pickpocket for Tanishi's Yakuza gang for awhile. Yahiko is rescued by Kenshin and moves into the Kamiya Dojo as a student.

Muto Kaname
Former Shishio follower. Flees prison with two of his colleagues. They are defeated by Yahiko and surrender.

N

Nakajo
Member of the Yaminobu and close friend of Otowa Hyoko.

Nagakura Shinpachi (1839-1915)
Shinsengumi Assistant Vice Commander. Lost a finger in the Ikedaya incident. In the Rurouni Kenshin universe, he fights the Battosai, but the match ends in a draw.

Nagaoka Mikio
Ne'er-do-well son of Nagaoka, a formal Shogunal vassal. Plotting to rob Akabeko, he forces Tsubame, daughter of his family's former retainer, to help him. Quite proficient at Kogen Itto-ryu, but loses to Yahiko anyway.

New Aoi-ya
The new Aoi-ya rebuilt after Fuji destroys the old one. The only difference is the addition of the word "New" on the sign.

Nishiwaki
A scoundrel employed by Hiruma Gohei to guard the Kiheikan when he heads off for the Kamiya Dojo. Nishiwaki proves utterly ineffective when faced with Kenshin.

O

Oguni Gensai:
Chief medic for the Kamiya Dojo and proprietor of the Oguni Clinic. Knew the doctor who formerly employed Megumi, and assists her after the Kanryu incident.

Oka Railway
Steam railway that began operating in Japan in 1872. It made the trip from Shinbashi (in Tokyo) to Yokohama in 54 minutes. In Rurouni Kenshin, it's used by Tsukayama Yutaro and family, Otowa Hyoko, and Inui Banjin.

Okita Soji (1842-1868)
Originally the leader of the 1st squad of the Shinsengumi. In the Rurouni Kenshin universe, he fights the Battosai, but the match ends in a draw.

Okon
Member of the Oniwabanshu. Works as a maid at Aoi-ya.

Okubo Toshimichi (1830-1878)
A real person. Minister of Home Affairs. One of the 3 great men of the Ishin, he was central to the Meiji government and introduced many modernization policies and laid the foundations of modern Japan. In the Rurouni Kenshin universe, he asks Kenshin to kill Shishio. Okubo himself is killed by Sojiro while awaiting Kenshin's answer. In reality, Okubo really was assassinated by a former Samurai from Ishikawa prefecture.

Oibore
A shellshocked old soldier. Loses his daughter and son during the Bakumatsu (Tomoe and Enishi). The shock turns him into a hermit.

Omasu
Member of the Oniwabanshu. Works as a maid at Aoi-ya. Has a child-like face.

Onidaoshi no Fudosawa
Crumbling yakuza. Tries to use his uncle, Tani Jusanro, to gain a piece of the silk industry. Plans to burn down the house of Higashidani, a competitor. Has 200 thugs with him, but they're all taken out by Sanosuke.

Oniwabanshu
Spies that protected the estates of Shogun and Daimyo. Composed of spies with superior combat skills. After the collapse of the Bakufu, four members of the Oniwabanshu form a team

with Aoshi called "Saikyo" (the strongest).

Oshige Baasan
Lives on the outskirts of Kyoto. Runs a tea house next to Arai Seiku's house. Owner of the pidgeon 'Runoichiban' that the Oniwabanshu use to communicate.

Otowa Hyoko
User of hidden weapons. Joins the Jinchu to avenge his friend. Possibly an opium addict. Loses to Yahiko.

P

Police Swordsmen
An elite group of police. All are exceptionally good with swords, having been chosen from among high-ranked officers, who are the police permitted to wear swords. They are violent and oppressive, but find themselves outmatched by Kenshin.

Q

R

Rakunin Cluster
Cluster of villages outside of Tokyo. A slum that naturally pops up due to the displacement of people caused by the Meiji revolution. Kenshin takes up residence here for awhile after Enishi's retribution.

Rensato no Murakami
Yaminobu assassin. Defeated by the Battosai.

Rokunin no Doshi ('the six comrades')
Group that appears in the Jinchu story arc. Lead by Yukishiro Enishi.

Room of Screams
Usui's room in Shishio's hideout. The walls and floor are decorated with a spooky eye theme.

Room Without Space
Sojiro's room in Shishio's hideout. It's a vast room, allowing Sojiro to exploit his speed.

Runoichiban
Messenger pigeon kept by Ms. Oshige. In the Kyoto region, the Iroha keep a total of 141 messenger pigeons, allowing the Kyoto Oniwabanshu to exchange information, literally as fast as the birds

can fly. This bird conveys the news of Iori's capture by Cho to Aoi-ya.

S

Sadojima Hoji
High ranking Meiji official who despairs in the new government and joins Shishio. No combat skills at all. An advisor and is in charge of acquiring troops and weapons. Surrenders along with Anji after Shishio's defeat. Seeing the backroom deals that are made in the legal system, he loses faith in the Meiji government for a second time, and kills himself in prison.

Sakura
Used as collateral on a debt, like Kenshin she is sold to slavers at a young age. Killed by bandits.

Sagara Sanosuke
Sanosuke works under the name 'Zanza' as a fighter-for-hire after the Sekihotai's destruction, but has a change of heart after losing to Kenshin. Later, he allies with Kenshin.

Sagara Sozo (1839-1868)
A real person. However, he was more dashing in real life than in the anime.

His real name was Kojima Shiro. He was originally not a samurai, but the son of an influential family. He left his hometown to participate in the Ishin. Originally from Shimousa, he studied Hirata Atsutane (an influential nationalistic scholar) and took part in the attack on the Bakufu. He was active during the chaos of that period, promoting the Ishin faction's promise to halve land taxes. In the end, he was accused with falsely representing the government and executed at 29.

Saikyo to iu na no Hana (the flower that is to be called 'the strongest')
Shinomori Aoshi's method of honoring the 4 slain Oniwabanshu. Instead of offering flowers he will instead commemorate them by defeating Kenshin and obtaining the title of "strongest". This leads Aoshi down a path to violence.

Saizuchi
The brains behind the 'Hagun'. Uses his clever tongue to deceive opponents. Fuji owes him his life. Knocked unconscious when Fuji lands on him after being defeated by Hiko Seijuro. Now secretly works as the government's foreign negotiator.

Sanjo Tsubame

A slightly timid girl the same age as Yahiko who works at Akabeko. The daughter of a samurai family, she's pressured into participating in the robbery of Akabeko by Mikio, the idiotic son of Nagaoka, a former Shogunal vassal (her family were originally retainers for the Nagaoka family). Yahiko comes to her rescue.

Saito Hajime

Based on a real person. Originally the leader of the 3rd squad of the Shinsengumi. Following the Ishin, he changes his name to Fujita Goro and becomes Assistant Inspector by way of serving as a police swordsman during the Seinan War. Working for Shishio's side, he fights Kenshin to a draw as a test of his strength. His philosophy is summed up in the three kanji 悪即斬 , which mean "Evil/Immediate/Execute". In other words, he's committed to destroying evil wherever he sees it. He is an expert in Gatotsu. After subduing Shishio, he vanishes, but isn't dead.

Sato-kun

Former student at the Kamiya Dojo. Picks a fight with the Hishimanji Gurentai while drunk, causing a lot of trouble for the dojo. Wears a hunting cap.

Sawagejo Cho

Member of the Juppon Gatana. Also called the 'sword hunter', he specializes in Saka Chuku Noto. In this technique, the sheath is flicked off the sword, then caught again on the blade, re-sheathing the sword. Uses Shakku's early blades, the Renbato. This sword consists of two blades stacked on top of one another so they look like a single blade. It makes two cuts very close to each other, so the wound can't be stitched and gets infected, killing the victim. Cho also keeps Shakku's Hakujin no Tachi hidden on his body. This sword behaves like a whip, so that even if the opponent dodges, Cho can redirect the blade. He uses this to perform the Orochi technique. Kenshin acquires the Sakabato Shinuchi, and defeats Cho with the Ryukansen Tsumuji. After being arrested, Cho exchanges his services as a spy for freedom, becoming one of Saito Hajime's men.

Sekihara Sae

Tae's identical twin sister. Manages Shirobeko by herself, since her father and sister are in Tokyo running Akabeko.

Sekihara Tae

Daughter of Akabeko's owner and Kaoru's friend. Always has a warm smile and an irrepressible personality. An avid collector of woodblock prints. She has a twin sister named Sae who works at Shirobeko, Akabeko's Kyoto franchise.

Senkaku

Shishio's underling who administers Shingetsu Village. Has a pointy shaved head. Uses two daggers. Although large and fast, he's no match for Kenshin's Ryushosen.

Shibata Ryujoetsukan

Dojo where Kaoru gives lessons 4 or 5 times a year. She has many fans there.

Shibumi

Secretary for the elder statesmen, and the fixer behind the 'Kurogasa incident'. Arranged assassinations in order to promote himself, but is killed by Saitu Hajime.

Shigekura Jubei

A Kyoto official. Assassinated by the Hitokiri Battosai.

Shikabane Doll

A stunning work of forgery. As Enishi is unable to kill young women, it is made in the shape of Kaoru, and used to make Kenshin and company believe that Kaoru is dead. It is made from the corpse of a young woman obtained at a graveyard.

Shikijo

An inner guard of the Edo Oniwabanshu. A heavily scarred strong-man. He was originally a spy from Satsuma who managed to sneak into Edo castle, but was defeated by the then 13 year-old Aoshi. After this, he joined the Oniwabanshu. He uses a secret Oniwabanshu formula to bulk up, but loses to Sanosuke. Killed with his comrades protecting Aoshi from Kanryu's Gatling gun.

Shimada Ichiro

A real person. Former samurai from Ishikawa prefecture who, with 7 comrades, attacked and killed Okubo while he was in his carriage. In Rurouni Kenshin, he attacks Okubo only to find that Sojiro has already killed him.

Shinichi Kozaburo

Cop who works at police headquarters. Cooperates with Yahiko to capture the escaped Kujiranami. After this joins the

Kamiya Dojo as a student.

Shingetsu Village

Fictional village located in Shizuoka prefecture near the outskirts of Numazu. The town is captured by Shishio's sect 2 years prior to the story arc, and is subsequently erased from all government maps. It is primarily administered by Senkaku, but Shishio returns once a year to make use of the volcanic springs. Kenshin frees the village, but its future remains uncertain.

Shinkoryu

A group of swordsman who are trying to revive traditional Japanese sword fighting and reject the use of bamboo swords (like those used in kendo). They have no decided form or technique, and members must simply meet the requirement of being "strong". They unsuccessfully attack the Kamiya Dojo after Kenshin rejects Raijuta's invitation to join them.

Shinomori Aoshi

Aoshi is a brilliant spy who became the leader of the Edo Oniwabanshu at just 15. He uses a Kodachi, or short sword. Works as Takeda Kanryu's bodyguard, but is defeated by Kenshin. Later, faces Kenshin again in an attempt to win the title of 'strongest man' for his fallen Oniwabanshu comrades. He learns the art of using two swords in an attempt to strengthen himself, but loses to Kenshin's Amakakeru Ryu no Hirameki. Now a devoted Zen practitioner.

Shiro

Member of the Oniwabanshu. Works as a cook at Aoi-ya.

Shinsengumi

a.k.a. "Wolves of Mibu". Group composed of the strongest of the pro-Bakufu swordsmen. They fought against the Ishin forces to protect Kyoto, but were defeated by the new government's modern weapons in the Boshin War. Saito is the former leader of the 3rd corps. Udo Jin-e is also a former member.

Shishio Makoto

Assassin active during the Bakumatsu. Succeeds Kenshin as 'Hitokiri Battosai'. Thought to have been burned to death by the government during the Boshin war, but in fact survived. Uses fire techniques. Bent on forming a huge army and toppling the Meiji government. As a result of his burns, he can only fight for 15 minutes at a time. Bursts into flames and dies during his fight with Kenshin.

Shirobeko

A restaurant in Kyoto that serves gyun-abe (a.k.a. sukiyaki). Tae's family home where Tae's big sister, Sae, lives. Kaoru and company stay there when they arrive in Kyoto. After Aoi-ya collapses, the Kyoto Oniwabanshu and Kenshin's group end up staying there.

Shu

Delinquent buddy of Sanosuke. Appears several times, but falls on hard luck in Chapter 153 of the Manga.

Shueiya

Gambling house to which Sanosuke invites Kenshin. It is here they meet Megumi, who's fleeing from Kanryu.

Spider's Web

The new form of opium that Kanryu forces Megumi to manufacture. This opium is unique in that it requires only half the raw materials as regular opium, but is twice as addictive. Kanryu intends to use this opium to acquire a vast fortune.

Sumita

Member of the Yaminobu. Uses a giant axe.

Sushin

Uheiren's gang of four, muscular body-guards. They are each masters of a weapon based on one of the four animal deities. They were originally a group of warriors known as the "Shijin". They are defeated by another gang of four: Saito Hajime, Shinomori Aoshi, Sagara Sanosuke, and Myojin Yahiko

T

Takani Megumi

Daughter of Takani Ryusei, a doctor from the Aizu province. Her family is scattered during the Aizu War. After this, she travels to Tokyo and begins assisting a certain doctor, 5 years before the story arc. This doctor manu-factures 'Spider's Web' opium with Takeda Kanryu, but Takeda kills him 3 years before the story opens. Megumi is confined by Kanryu and forced to produced opium, but is later freed by Kenshin and company. She then begins working at Gensai-sensei's clinic.

Takani Ryusei

A doctor from the Aizu province. His family had a tradition of producing doc-tors. He abruptly left Aizu to study Western medicine, moving his entire household to Nagasaki. This demonstrates his devotion to medicine and his patients. About the time he's permitted to re-enter Aizu, the Meiji Ishin begins, and Takani is killed in the Aizu War.

Takasugi Shinsaku (1839-67)
A real person. Another significant Choshu leader. Forms the Kihei-tai.

Tatsumi
Leader of the Yaminobu. Uses Muteki-ryu.

Takeda Kanryu
Appears to be a young businessman, but in reality is a shady opium dealer. Employs the Oniwabanshu and a private army as bodyguards. Hoping to make a killing as an arms merchant, he acquires Gatling guns, one of which he uses to destroy the Oniwabanshu. Defeated by Kenshin and arrested.

Tani Jusanro
Formerly an Ishin activist from Choshu. Currently a leader in the Japanese army, but has fallen into corruption. Initially targeted by Kurogasa. Later, goes to Shinshu on behalf of his nephew, who's attempting to acquire interests in silk production, but instead receives a painful experience courtesy of Sanosuke.

Tanishi
Head of the Kanto Shueigumi yakuza. Adopts the orphaned Yahiko and forces him to steal to earn his meals. He is persuaded to release Yahiko by Kenshin's intimidating gaze.

Tasuke
An orphan who lived at Jurakuji. Often bullied Goro.

Tokugawa Bakufu (1603-1867)
a.k.a. Tokugawa Shogunate. The feudal government headed by the Tokugawa family that ruled Japan prior to the Meiji Ishin. The period of Bakufu rule is referred to as the Edo Period, because Japan's capital was moved to Edo (now Tokyo).

Tsubaki
Organized the orphans who lived at Jurakuji. Her father, the former town headman, supported the Bakufu during the Boshin war. Was very fond of Anji.

Tsukioka Katsuhiro
An old friend of Sanosuke from the Sekihotai. Works as a woodblock artist under the name of Tsukioka Tsunan after the Sekihotai is dismantled. His plans to commit a terrorist attack on the

government with a bomb are frustrated by Kenshin. Later quits art and founds a newspaper to expose government attrocities. Has a dark personality, and builds bombs as a hobby.

Tsukayama Yutaro

A young man who is enamored with Raijuta's strength. Rebels against his merchant father. His right hand is wounded when he's betrayed by Raijuta. Has to go to Germany to have his hand treated. Becomes the Kamiya Dojo's second student, and shows great aptitude.

Tsukayama Yuzaemon

Trader. Yutaro's father. Of samurai ancestry, but uses his sword expertise as a sword dealer, selling to foreign clients. Yuzaemon becomes Raijuta's patron after the latter saves him from an assailent, but this was actually set up by Raijuta in the first place.

Todo Heisuke (1844-1867)

Shinsengumi Assistant Vice Commander. Cut on the brow during the Ikedaya incident.

Tomo

Delinquent buddy and gambling partner of Sanosuke. Seriously injured by Beshimi.

U

Udo Jin-e

Jin-e is a master swordsman who uses the Nikaido Heiho style. He is a ruthless killer who targets former Ishin activists that are now prominent politicians and bureaucrats, to whom he sends formal challenges before killing. When he first appeared in Kyoto during the Bakumatsu, he worked for the Shinsengumi. He killed countless Ishin activists, but because he killed needlessly, the Shinsengumi tried to execute him. Jin-e fled, and some months later showed up on the opposite side of the conflict, working for the Ishin. He has a remarkably track record, having never failed a single attempted assassination during his 10 year nationwide killing spree. Jin-e kidnaps Kaoru to provoke Kenshin to revert to his 'Hitokiri Battosai' persona. Disabled by Kenshin's Soryusen attack, Jin-e ultimately kills himself, leaving behind the ominous words: 'Once a killer, always a killer.'

U Heiren

Enishi's No .2 man. His strategy and management enabled Enishi's business to thrive. Has ambitions to be more than just Enishi's right-hand man. No combat skills.

Ujiki

The Assistant Inspector of the Police Swordsmen. Originally from Satsuma. Treacherous, and holds himself in high regard due to his elite status as a master of Jigen-ryu. Turns violent while attempting to bust Kenshin for his violation of the sword prohibition, but predictably is no match for the former hitokiri.

Uonuma Usui

Second in command of the Juppon Gatana. Formerly a killer for the Bakufu, he loses his eyes in a battle with Shishio. From this he gains the ability of 'mind's eye'. His ostensible reason for joining Shishio is that he's waiting for a chance to kill him, but actually knows that he'd never win. Killed by Saito Hajime's 'Gatotsu Zeroshiki'.

Uramura

The Chief of Police in the are where the Kamiya Dojo is located. Objects to Ujiki's violence. Puts up with Kenshin's violation of the sword prohibition, perhaps due to Yamagata's influence. Both helped by and helps out Kenshin and company. Has a wife and one daughter.

V

Villa

A villa in Yokohama. Temporary residence of Enishi and his 6 cohorts in their quest for Jinchu.

W

White Cloak

The symbol of Hiten Mitsurugi-Ryu's successors. It includes a heavy colar (over 37kg!) that acts sort of like a giant spring, pushing against the wearer's muscles. It's purpose is to suppress the power of the Hiten Mitsurugi-Ryu successors, and is an ongoing tradition of the style, like the title of Hiko Seijuro.

X

Y

Yakuzatai

A division of Takeda Kanryu's private army.

Yamagata Aritomo (1838-

1922)

A historical figure. Former commander of the Kihei-tai, during the Rurouni Kenshin story arc, he is commander of the Japanese Army. Pays a visit on Kenshin during the false Battosai incident. Having worked for the Meiji government once as an assassin, Kenshin turns down Yamagata's offer for further employment.

Yamayoshi Morisuke (1835-1902)

Real person from Fukushima prefecture. Last person to speak with Okubo. In Rurouni Kenshin, he tells Kenshin about Okubo's ideals.

Yaminobu

A group of pro-Bakufu assassins. They become a problem when they decide to go after the Hitokiri Battosai, but are defeated.

Yatsume Ichizoku

Family of gold-miners. Their secret technique of "body purification" allows them to prosper, but when their gold vein is depleted, they move to Hokkaido.

Yatsume Mumyoi

Is heard, but not seen. Joins the Jinchu to kill Kenshin, who has seen his true form. Belonged to the Yaminobu. Defeated by Saito Hajime.

Yatsume no Jintaiseisei

A secret technique born of the competition between gold miners. Gold bracelets are fit around the arms and legs of newborn children. As the child grows, the number of bracelets is increased, stretching their arms and legs and giving them an advantage is the subterranean caves caverns.

Yukishiro Enishi

Brother-in-law of Himura Kenshin. Crosses over to Shanghai, where he becomes a mafia boss, handing all black-market weapons that arrive via the continent. Shishio's battleship was provided by Enishi. Begins the 'Jinchu' campaign of revenge against the Battosai (Kenshin) over the death of his sister. Specializes in Watojutsu Enishi's never-ending hatred of Kenshin, keeps him in a constant state of heightened tension. As a result, his nervous system never rests, and his nerves have thickened allowing Enishi to move much faster than normal people. This condition is called Kyokei Myaku.

Yukishiro Tomoe

Himura Kenshin's wife and Enishi's younger sister. Plans to kill Kenshin to avenge her fiancé, but falls for him after getting to know him. Her efforts to protect Kenshin get her killed along with Tatsumi.

Yukyuzan Anji

3rd most powerful member of the Juppon Gatana. A former Buddhist priest who develops the Futae no Kiwami for 'salvation'. During the early Meiji backlash against Buddhism, his temple is destroyed and along with it an orphan he's caring for. Turns himself in to the police after losing to Sanosuke, and works off his crimes in Hokkaido.

Z

Zankanjo

A notice of challenge sent by the assassin "Kurogasa" to the politicians he's about to kill.

Swords created by Arai Shakku

Sakabato

The sword Kenshin receives from Arai Shakku after retiring from the hitokiri business. It cannot cut when wielded normally since the cutting edge of the blade is on the side that would normally be the back.

The sword is broken in Shingetsu Village during the fight with Seta Sojiro. It is actually the twin of the superior Sakabato Shinuchi.

Sakabato Shinuchi

Arai Shakku always made two of each sword. In the case of the Sakabato, he gave one to Kenshin, but retained the other, called the 'Shinuchi'. This sword was his final creation and was donated to a shrine. Kenshin receives this sword when the original Sakabato is destroyed.

Renbato

One of Arai Shakku early killer blades. It consists of two blades stacked on top of one another so they look like a single blade. It's very difficult to treat Renbato wounds because the sword makes two cuts very close to each other, so the wound often gets infected killing the victim. Possessed by Cho, but Kenshin destroys it.

Hakujin no Tachi

One of Arai Shakku later killer blades. It is a blade made of steel pounded as thinly as physically possible, with a slight weight at the tip. This allows the blade to be controlled with a flick of the wrist. Possessed by Cho.

Mugenjin

Arai Shakku's final killer blade and Shishio's weapon. Its capacity to kill and wound is preserved by its partially serrated edge, allowing it to be used continuously without sharpening.

Weapons of the Juppon Gatana

Kotetsu

One of the 31 great swords. It is a weapon of exceptional beauty, the mere sight of which causes any sword expert worth his/her salt to burn with desire. This is the sword that Sojiro uses to break Kenshin's Sakabato, although the Kotetsu is also severely damaged in the process.

Rengoku

A huge battleship. Shishio spends over half of his assets to purchase it from Yukishiro. It used Armstrong cannons and Gatling guns, making it one of the most powerful warships in Japan. Shishio planned to use the Rengoku to bombard Tokyo, but Sanosuke blows it up.

Tinbe to Rochin

A pair of weapons that Usui uses. Historically, these weapons were used by the royalty of the Ryukyu Islands. The Tinbe is a tortoise-shell shield. It uses the natural roundness of the shell to deflect enemy attacks and block their line of sight. The Rochin is a short spear.

Okusari Gama

Kamatari's weapon of choice. It combines a heavy-duty okama ('big sickle') with a weighted chain.

Kiku Ichimonji Norimune

Sojiro's beloved sword. A truly remarkable blade that surpasses even Japan's most famous blades. Shattered by Kenshin's Amakakeru Ryu no Hirameki.

Wakizashi

The short sword Sojiro uses to kill his abusive family. He received it from Shishio and returns it upon deciding to part ways with his mentor.

Weapons of the Oniwabanshu

Kodachi

Shinomori Aoshi's weapon. While shorter and less lethal than a normal katana, its speed makes it excellent for defense. Aoshi usually uses this sword in place of a shield while attacking with kempo techniques, but the Kodachi comes into play during his special moves, such as the Kaiten Kenbu.

Shikomi Nunchaku

A pair of nunchaku Kashiwazaki Nenji carries around disguised as a walking stick. Misao borrows them to stop Cho.

Tonfa

Kashiwazaki 'Okina' Nenji's weapons. They are made of steel, but nonetheless Aoshi is able to cut through them with his Onmyo Kosa technique.

Enkei Shuriken

Weapon used by Omasu of the Kyoto

Oniwabanshu. She can throw the shields she wears on both hands like shuriken.

Kunoji Shuriken
Weapon used by Okon of the Kyoto Oniwabanshu. A boomerang-shaped shuriken she wears on her back.

Kotewa Shuriken
Weapon used by Kuro and Shiro of the Kyoto Oniwabanshu. Their gauntlets are made up of numerous rings, which they can detach and throw at enemies.

The 3 Great Weapons of the Bakumatsu

Gatling Gun
Weapon used by Takeda Kanryu to wipe out the Oniwabanshu. One of the great imported weapons of the Bakumatsu period.

Armstrong Breech-loading Cannon
A powerful Western weapon imported into Japan around the Bakumatsu period. In addition to being standard equipment on the Rengoku, The Armstrong cannon is also used by Kujiranami in place of his missing arm.

CSS Stonewall
An iron-clad battleship similar to the Rengoku. This was an actual ship originally owned by the Confederate Navy. After the Civil War, it was sold to Japan where it was renamed the Kotetsu, and later the Azuma. It ended up in the ownership of the pro-Ishin forces, who used it as part of their efforts to crush the remnant Bakufu supporters after the Boshin War.

The Jinchu Arc

Iwanbo
Originally thought to be a member of the Juppon Gatana, it's actually a mechanical doll controlled from the inside by Gein. Its soft exterior can absorb any physical attack.

Nigo Iwanbo
The second Iwanbo created by Gein after the first one is destroyed. He creates it to destroy the Maekawa Dojo.

Ogata Sakuretsudan
The bomb hidden inside the second Iwanbo. It is meant to blow up the Maekawa Dojo, but thanks to Sanosuke's quick thinking, it only man-

ages to do half the job.

Sango Iwanbo Moshugata

The first real 'combat' Iwanbo. Used to attack Kenshin. It can absorb attacks (Shogeki Kyushu Karakuri), and is equipped with universal joints (Jiyukansetsu Karakuri). Gein can also eject part of the suit (Jizai Dacchaku Karakuri).

Jizai Dacchaku Karakuri

A defense feature of the Sango Iwanbo. Part of the suit can be dumped, leaving the super-elastic rubber surface and steel control cables. However, this is very difficult to do.

Jiyukansetsu Karakuri

A feature of the Sango Iwanbo. All of its joints can rotate freely.

Shogeki Kyushu Karakuri

A defense feature of the Sango Iwanbo. The Iwanbo's thick exterior can absorb any attacks.

Taishi Totsusei Soko Karakuri

A defense feature of the Sango Iwanbo. A flexible but strong web of interlaced steel fibers make it impervious to all piercing attacks.

Tekko

Literally means 'iron plating'. Wristbands worn by Inui Banjin. The Tekko can deflect the strongest swords and are thick enough to block even bullets. He obtains them from the black market via Enishi's connections.

Shin Muteki Tekko

Inui Banjin's 'invincible' new Tekko boast more refined performance and configuration than the previous model.

Baika Chuzen

Weapon that fires metal spears out of six barrels using a powerful spring. Used by Otowa Hyoko and his bosom buddy Nakajo.

Kasui Busuen

One of Otowa Hyoko's secret weapons. It reacts with water, creating a poison that numbs the limbs for 4 or 5 minutes. Useful for effecting escapes or as a distraction.

Bishamonken

Another of Otowa's weapons, which he acquires in the Jinchu campaign. He has magnetized his blade by keeping it in a magnetic sheath. Using the blade together with Bishamonpun (Bishamon powder) gives the blade the ability to automatically 'track' its target.

Bishamonpun
Powder that gives the Bishamonken its true power. Actually iron sand.

Rikudoko
Otowa's ultimate weapon. Disguised as an eccentric decorative garment. Hard to recognize as a weapon since it's hidden in plain sight. Used to skewer carelessly attacking opponents.

Bandan Raiho
Bombs that Yatsume receives from Enishi in Jinchu campaign. These bombs were invented in China during the Ming dynasty and consist of a pottery shell filled with gunpowder and a detonator charge. Can be detonated by stepping on them or with a tripwire. Yatsume uses them to create perimeters.

Zankosen
Diamond dust impregnated metal wire that Gein uses. A mere touch can slice through flesh and even bone.

Renshagata Custom Grenade Launcher
New weapon used by Kujiranami when he escapes. What it lacks in firepower

and range, it compensates for in its high rate of fire.

Chenron Daito
Weapon belonging to Seiryu of the Sushin. Its length and Seiryu's quick reactions allow him to deliver counter-thrusts when his enemy least expects it.

Chucha Soengimu
Weapon belonging to Suzaku of the Sushin. A Chinese style short sword used in Nitto-ryu (two-sword) techniques.

Yunmo Seikuan
Weapon belonging to Genbu of the Sushin. Looks like a normal staff, but can be separated into freely moving sections for defensive use.

Tekki
Weapon belonging to Byakko of the Sushin used to perform backhand blows. Look like rugged armlets, but are actually weapons.

Miscellaneous

Mokuho
A simple cannon that was used in Japan until the beginning of the Bakumatsu period. The barrel was made of oak, and

it fired clay projectiles. It was considerably less powerful than a normal cannon. Kenshin encounters one of these, and actually chops its cannonball in half.

Zanbato

A huge sword used during Japan's Sengoku period to take down mounted soldiers, horse and all. Sanosuke's zanbato has lost its edge, and is therefore used more as a bludgeon than a sword. Kenshin breaks this sword, but it reappears, after some hasty repairs, in the Jinchu arc. Sanosuke uses it to deflect a shot from the Armstrong cannon, only to have it shatter on Banjin's upgraded Tekko.

Suntetsu

A weapon concealed in the palm of the hand and exposed when punching to deal extra damage. The drunk activist uses one of these against Sanosuke to no effect.

Soshinto

Used by one of the Shinko-ryu (Raijuta's lackey). Has a blade attached to both ends of the hilt.

Saku Retsudan

Secretly constructed by Tsunan

Tsukioka as a terrorist weapon. After his terrorist plot crumbles, he develops an improved version and gives it to Sanosuke as a parting gift. It plays a key role in sinking the Rengoku.

Kusari Gama

One of Akamatsu Arundo's weapons. The weapon's strong points are the weight attached to the chain and the sickle's wave attack, but Akamatsu can't seem to land either.

Shikomi Bundo

One of Akamatsu Arundo's weapons. He uses this concealed weighted chain to stun and strangle opponents.

Nigiri Kaiken

Senkaku's weapon. These are daggers he holds in both hands and uses to carve up enemies.

Rensato

Murakami's weapon. Consists of two blades connected with a chain. Uses one blade and the chain to stop his enemies, and the other blade to attack.

Hiten Mitsurugi-ryu

An ancient fighting style that stretches back to Japan's Sengoku period and is optimized for taking on multiple opponents. Its purpose is protecting people from the strife of the ages. The successor of its most secret technique takes on the name of Hiko Seijuro. The current Hiko Seijuro is the 14th successor.

Amakakeru Ryu no Hirameki

The most secret Hiten Mitsurugi-ryu technique. Relies on the wielder's will to live to produce superhuman speed. This invincible technique embodies the philosophy of the Hiten Mitsurugi-ryu style.

Kuzuryusen

Learned in the process of initiation into the Amakakeru Ryu no Hirameki technique, the Kuzuryusen exploits the god-like speed of Hiten Mitsurugi-ryu to its fullest. Using it, the attacker strikes nine points on the opponent simultaneously, making it impossible to block. In all schools of the sword arts, there are 9 vital target areas which students are trained to protect. By attacking all 9 at once, this technique assures that no matter what style the opponent is using, s/he won't be able to block the blow. Hiko Seijuro's signature technique.

Soryusen

A two-stage attack developed to overcome the vulnerability of sword-drawing techniques. After the initial sword attack, a second blow is landed with the scabbard.

Soryusen Ikazuchi

The opposite of the Soryusen above, the sword attack follows the first blow, landed with the scabbard.

Doryusen

The sword is used to strike the ground, driving off the foe with a shower of pebbles and dirt. Used frequently by raiders during the Bakumatsu.

Hiryusen

The sword is launched out of its sheath, striking the enemy with the hilt. Allows a ranged attack, but can only be performed once.

Ryukansen

The defender spins out of the way of the opponent's attack, then attacks from behind.

Ryukansen Arashi
Ryukansen with a somersault added to the attack.

Ryukansen Kogarashi
Another Ryukansen variation.

Ryukansen Tsumuji
Ryukansen incorporating a reverse blow.

Ryushosen
The flat of the blade is used to uppercut the opponent in the chin. Originally this was a more lethal technique, as the blade was used.

Ryusosen
Showers the opponent with multiple blows.

Ryusosen Garami
A variation of the Ryusosen attack.

Ryutsuisen
The attacker leaps into the air and delivers a crushing blow from above. This is the first special technique we see Kenshin use (used on Hiruma Gohei).

Ryutsuisen Zan

An exceptionally brutal technique. The attacker leaps into the air and stabs downward from above. Used to dispatch Shigekura Jubei.

Ryumeisen
A super-sonic sword-sheathing technique. Creates a small sonic boom with the hand-guard, temporarily deafening the opponent.

Kamiya Kasshin-ryu

Style developed by Kamiya Jiro at the beginning of the Meiji period. He sought to use the sword as a means of drawing out people's potential, rather than as weapons of death. Its main strategy is to control rather than kill the opponent.

Hiza Hishigi
A disabling blow with the hilt of the sword to the opponent's knee. Breaks the knee, rendering the opponent unable to fight.

Ogi no Mamori Hadome
The Kamiya Kasshin-ryu's secret technique. Unlike regular empty-handed sword-taking techniques, in this technique the defender keeps his/her own ´ sword while redirecting the attacker's strength.

Ogi no Seme Hawatari

Attack derived from the Hadome. The more quickly it is performed, the more of the opponent's own strength is redirected back against him/her.

Ogi no Kiwami Hadachi

The ultimate of Kamiya Kasshin-ryu's secret techniques. The defender catches and shatters the opponent's blade with bare hands.

Sagara Sanosuke's Techniques

Sanju no Kiwami

Special technique created by Yukyuzan Anji and learned by Sanosuke. Two punches are delivered in short interval, so that the second punch lands before the first punch has rebounded. This technique transmits the punch's power with no resistance, and is strong enough to pulverize rocks.

Sanju no Kiwami

After performing the Futae no Kiwami, the fingers are snapped open to deliver one more impact. Allows Sanosuke to defeat Anji, but breaks his own right hand in the process.

Udo Jin-e's Techniques

Nikaido Heiho

Jin-e's sword-fighting style. It is divided into three stages, represented by the ideographs for '1' (一), '8' (八) and '10' (十).

Shin no Ippo

A Nikaido Heiho technique that uses hypnotism. Jin-e focuses his willpower through his eyes, immobilizing opponents. Also known by the name 'Isukumi'. By intensifying this technique, Jin-e can paralyze his victim's lungs, causing death by suffocation.

Hyoki no Jutsu

The complement to the Shin no Ippo technique. Jin-e hypnotizes himself to bring out all of his potential. He uses this to escape the Shinsengumi, and during his battle with Kenshin.

Haishato

One of Jin-e's techniques. It is essentially a feint in which he switches his blade from his right to left hand behind his back before attacking.

Shinomori Aoshi's Techniques

Onmyo Kosa

Technique for two short swords. The swords are crossed, and are able to cut through even steel.

Onmyo Hasshi

Technique for two short swords. The first sword blocks the opponent's view of the second sword, which he throws in precisely the same trajectory.

Kaiten Kenbu

Aoshi combines kempo moves with short-sword techniques to create a lethal dance. He can vary the speed of the attack at will, and his fluid movement keeps his opponent at bay. Judging by the wounds it inflicts, it appears to land 3 successive blows.

Kaiten Kenbu Rokuren

Aoshi's signature move. Inflicts six (2 blades x 3 revolutions) blindingly fast attacks. His ability to spin either right or left and the six instantaneous cuts are what make it so lethal.

Gokojuji

Technique for two short swords. Aoshi crosses his blades and severs his oppo-nent's carotid artery.

Ryusui no Ugoki

The foundation of the Kodachi Nitto Ryu style and Aoshi's favored technique. He uses his fluid movements to disorient his opponent.

Oniwabanshu Techniques

Rasenbyo

One of Beshimi's weapons. He throws darts that have a spiral shape, allowing them to spin very rapidly.

Dokusatsu Rasenbyo

One of Beshimi's weapons. He adds poison to his throwing darts, making them even more dangerous. Once hit, the victim has only an hour to live.

Kaen Toiki

Hyottoko's signature technique. He can become a human flame-thrower by regurgitating oil from a bag he keeps in his stomach and igniting it with his flinty teeth. He loses to Sanosuke, who manages to yank out the oil bag.

Shinwan no Jutsu

Hannya's signature technique. He has tattooed both his arms, creating the illusion that they are shorter and thicker than they actually are. This interferes with the eye's ability to judge their length, and gives the impression that they stretch and lengthen. The technique is perfect for Hannya, who is rail-thin and favors evasion.

Kansatsu Tobikunai

A techniques used by Misao. Although she throws 8 kunai (throwing knives) simultaneously in this attack, it isn't very strong.

Ikari no Kecho Keri

A technique Misao uses when angry. Very effective against weak or unprepared opponents.

Ensatsu Gokokon

Okina's signature move. He delivers a blow at close range using all his body weight.

Isurugi Raijuta's Techniques

Izuna

A sword technique Raijuta finds in an ancient martial-arts manual and spends 10 years learning. He creates a vacuum in the air with his sword. This vacuum creates a pressure wave that is capable of cutting. This technique was apparently inspired by a natural phenomenon called 'kamaitachi' (weasel's slash) which is reported to occur in certain parts of Japan. It causes cuts to appear on people's skin for no apparent reason. The official explanation is vacuums created by cyclones, but some victims claim they were attacked by sickle-wielding weasels. (Note: an Izuna is a mythical, fox-like creature, and also the name of a real type of weasel.)

Mato Izuna

Another Izuna technique. A vacuum trails behind the tip of his sword, increasing the sting of its cut. He can use this to produce a very real cut, even with a bamboo sword.

Tobi Izuna

The ultimate Izuna technique. Raijuta sends pressure waves flying at his opponents. Capable of ranged attacks.

Saito Hajime's Techniques

Gatotsu

Saito's signature technique. It's a refined form of the Shinsengumi

Hirazugi technique and is performed with the left hand. He uses different variations depending on the situation.

Gatotsu Isshiki
The standard, most conservative attack.

Gatotsu Nishiki
A strong downward thrust, for use when Saito has the high ground.

Gatotsu Sanshiki
An upward thrust, for use when Saito's opponent has the high ground.

Gatotsu Zeroshiki
The Gatotsu's ultimate weapon. A close range technique, using thrusts delivered with the upper-body only. He holds this technique back for the final confrontation with Kenshin, but uses it on Usui after suffering injuries to both legs.

Hirazugi
Technique invented by Hijikata Toshizo, the Shinsengumi's deputy leader. Even if the thrusting attack misses, it can be followed immediately by a horizontal slash. Perfected in Saito's Gatotsu.

Techniques of the Juppon Gatana

Sakasa Kuchu Noto
This is a show technique in which the Juppon Gatana flick the sheaths off their swords, then catching them again on the blade, re-sheathing their swords. Cho intimidates Seiku by snagging Iori on his sheath while doing this.

Garyu Orochi
Cho's technique. He manipulates his sword, the Hakujin no Tachi, so that it wriggles like a snake.

Futae no Kiwami
Special technique Yukyuzan Anji develops in the course of his quest for "salvation". Two punches are delivered in a short interval, so that any opposing shock is transformed into destructive power. When they meet in the mountains, Anji agrees to teach Sanosuke the technique on the condition that he learn it in just one week.

Toate
An application of the Futae no Kiwami. Allows a ranged attack by transmitting the Futae no Kiwami through a sword and into the ground.

Boken Bogyaku Hyakka Ryoran

Usui's technique. He performs successive attacks alternating between a spear and a weight attached to its handle.

Hiku Happa

Henya's technique. By starving himself down to skin and bones, he is able to achieve flight using explosives and a special costume. He uses his lofty position to rain down attacks with impunity. Although this exploits the blind-spot all people have above their heads, he too suffers from the same blind-spot.

Midare Benten

Honjo Kamatari's signature technique. He/she (ahem) whirls both his/her scythe and the weight attached to its chain simultaneously, chopping up anything that gets near her…er…him. Interestingly, the weapon's name, Ogama, is kind of similar to'okama', the Japanese word for a transvestite, or effeminate man. Pun intended? (Note: Benten is the Japanese version of the Hindu goddess Sarasvati, who is the diety of art, dancing and music.)

Benten Mawashi

One of Honjo's techniques. If her scythe's handle breaks, she can wrap the chain around its attached weight and spin it with her scythe.

Shukuchi

Sojiro's super-speedy technique. He uses the elastic strength of his legs to suddenly accelerate from low speed to his top speed, instantly closing on his opponent. He moves so quickly, that it seems as if the distance between him and his opponent has physically shrunk. His speed is so great, it evades even the Kuzuryusen.

Shuntensatsu

Technique named by Sojiro. He attacks with a sword-drawing technique directly from Shukuchi. This attack is foiled by a Amakakeru Ryu no Hirameki combination.

Shishio Makoto's Techniques

Ichi no Hiken Homuradama

One of Shishio's techniques. He can produce sparks and flames from the tip of his sword, the Mugenjin, which is imbued with human fat. Cuts and burns his opponents simultaneously.

Ni no Hiken Gurenkaina
One of Shishio's techniques. Uses the Homuradama to ignite gunpowder hidden in his arm-guards.

Tsui no Hiken Kaguzuchi
Shishio unleashes all of Mugenjin's incendiary power.

Muteki-ryu
A synthesis of martial arts from many eras and countries. Used by Inui Banjin and his master Tatsumi. The incorporation of armor can further enhance this style.

Kofubaku
A Muteki-ryu technique and Tatsumi's signature attack. Places a blow directly on the throat. Looks something like the Lariat, or Axe Bomber move from professional wrestling.

Raijin Guruma
A Muteki-ryu technique and one of Inui's signature attacks. He performs a mid-air spin, striking with his entire body. It completely destroys the Kamiya Dojo's front gate.

Ashura Sai
A Muteki-Ryu technique and one of Inui's signature attacks. A combined 3-stage attack. (Note: Ashuras are super-natural beings in Hindu/Buddhist mythology.)

Gofubaku
A Muteki-Ryu technique and one of Inui's signature attacks. It's just slightly different from Tatsumi's Kofubaku.

Watojutsu
A sword style from the late Ming era. The swords used by Japanese pirates were imported into mainland China and evolved into the Wato (Wo Dao) sword. This style fuses the speed and sharpness of Japanese blades with the grace and power of mainland martial arts. This is Enishi's signature style.

Shuki Tosei
Double attack combining a sword slash and a kick.

Kaishi Tosei
Enishi stops the attacker's blow with his scabbard, using the impact to add momentum to his counter-attack.

Shoha Tosei
Enishi holds the Wato in one hand and uses the palm of the other to press on the ridge, increasing the force of the slash.

Choten Tosei
Enishi performs a kick using the Wato

as an anchor. There is a cord attached to the scabbard, allowing him to bring it into the attack instantly.

Kofuku Zettosei
The ultimate Wato technique. Enishi begins in a low crouch, then lunges, driving the Wato into his victim's chest. It is very effective against the Amakakeru Ryu no Hirameki, and overcomes Kenshin.

Senran Tosei
Enishi begins in a low crouch, then spins rapidly towards his opponent, blade extended.

Shikku Tosei
Enishi jumps, then just as he's about to drop back to earth, he uses thrust generated by a kick to cancel his downward momentum, allowing him to seem to sprint through mid-air. A 'double-jump' in other words.

Gotsui Tosei
Enishi skewers and lifts his opponent over his head, before smashing the hapless victim to the ground.

Kyokei Myaku
The name for Yukishiro Enishi's medical condition. His bloated nerves give him a reaction time noticeably quicker than that of normal people.

Other Techniques

Ukiashi Otoshi
A Kogen Itto-ryu technique that Nagaoka Mikio uses. It targets the lower legs -the Achilles' heel of sword techniques- but is no match for Yahiko's weapon-breaking technique.

Shirahadori
One of the few empty-handed techniques in the 500 or so schools of sword fighting. Kenshin uses it twice while fighting Aoshi.

Miyo Mimane Ryutsuisen
Yahiko learns Kenshin's Ryutsuisen by watching and is able to use it. In his fight against Henya, he uses a door to 'surf' the blast of Henya's bombs to gain enough altitude to use this technique. It seems Yahiko didn't think through the landing bit very well, but he defeats Henya nonetheless.

Modoshi Giri
If a cut is made very delicately, the halves of whatever was cut can be put back together, restoring the object as if nothing happened. This technique can

only be performed by an expert swordsperson using an excellent blade. Kenshin tries this technique with one of the kitchen knives produced by Arai Seiku's to check the quality of the blade.

Senwan Geki
One of Iwanbo's techniques that takes advantage of his flexible joints. He twists his arm up, allowing him to perform a corkscrew punch.

Senshinwan Geki
Iwanbo's ultimate technique. Like the Senwan Geki, but even his fingers spin.

Gehokuri Itojutsu Kikahachi Hojin
Gein's ultimate technique. Boxes in his opponent with steel wire impregnated with highly refined oil. He ignites the wire and burns his opponent to death.

Ryushosen Modoki
ÅF Yahiko learns Kenshin's Ryushosen by watching and makes use of it. He succeeds in inflicting some damage to Kujiranami's right hand.

Oyaji no Tatsumaki
One of Kamishimoemon's techniques. Causes opponents to sail spinning through the air.

Oyaji no Atsukitamashii
One of Kamishimoemon's techniques. Kamishimoemon shoots a lump of burning tobacco out of his pipe into his opponent's face.

Oni Taoshi
Fudosawa's specialty. Although this open-handed blow has humiliated countless sumo wrestlers, it doesn't even phase Sanosuke.

Paafu Chie Mukun
Technique used by Byakko of the Sushin. By using the most appropriate form for different target areas, this technique can even be used effectively again real tigers.

KEYWORD INDEX

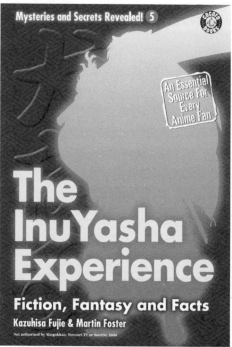

The tale of InuYasha, a mystical half-demon, and Kagome, a schoolgirl transported back in time from present-day Tokyo, is one of anime biggest hits. Set in Japan's ancient Era of Warring States, when demons and magic ruled, InuYasha is the story of a quest to find the shards of the broken Shikon jewel, and by doing so bring peace to the land and love to the protagonist and his modern-day princess.

192 pages packed with secrets, subplots, character traits, hidden meanings, behind-the-scenes gossip and little-known facts, **The InuYasha Experience** opens up a whole new world that anime fans never knew existed. Find out who did what when and why in one of the most popular anime ever released on either side of the Pacific!

Cosplay Girls
Japan's Live
Animation Heroines

All over Japan, hard-core fans of anime, games and manga are hitting the streets in their latest cosplay outfits - especially girls! And cosplay is now catching on fast overseas. Inside Cosplay Girls you'll find tough street-fighting chicks, emerald-haired princesses, spunky school girls and faux-fur kittens. This full-color glossy book is also packed with info on the characters they portray, how to pose, and methods of making and wearing costumes. As well as a fun guide to games, manga and anime big in Japan, Cosplay Girls also highlights the creative powers of Japanese otaku girls.

Secrets of the Ninja
Their Training,
Tools and Techniques

Now you see them, now you don't. Peek inside the ninja's world and discover the skills, weapons, and ingenious tricks that made these men and women feared and revered for centuries. Learn ninja techniques for meditation, stealth and fighting dirty. Study their diet, ancient codes, workout and accupressure points. With Secrets of the Ninja, unravel the many mysteries of the enigmatic ninja and find out what it really meant to be one in old Japan.

$19.95   ISBN 0-9723124-6-3